Portraits of War

In early 2003, the Detroit Free Press and Knight Ridder newspapers sent a writer and an artist to the Middle East, to tell the story of the war in Iraq. One sketch at a time.

They told the stories of everyday people – soldiers and civilians, the men, women and children – caught in the cross fire of the Iraq war.

Writer Jeff Seidel and artist Richard Johnson filed from four countries – Qatar, Bahrain, Kuwait and Iraq. They spent time at Central Command in Doha, Qatar, meeting the men and women who would run the war. They traveled aboard the USS Abraham Lincoln, an aircraft carrier in the Persian Gulf. During the war, they were embedded with the Marines. They ate with them, slept with them and rode across the Iraqi border with the men and women of the 6th Engineer Support Battalion.

Through Johnson's portraits and Seidel's profiles, the complexity of this war begins to emerge at the most human level: the hope, horror, comedy, death, fear, honor, courage and sacrifice.

Detroit Free Press

>KNIGHT RIDDER>

Detroit Free Press

>KNIGHT RIDDER>

600 W. Fort St.
Detroit, MI 48226
www.freep.com

© 2003 by Detroit Free Press.

Other recent books by the Free Press:

Razor Sharp:	Fishing Michigan
Drew Sharp	Hockey Gods
Hang 10	Motoons:
Time Frames	Mike Thompson
The Detroit Almanac	Ernie Harwell:
HeartSmart Kids	Stories From
Cookbook	My Life in Baseball
State of Glory	Corner to Copa
The Corner	Century of Champions
PC@Home	Yaklennium
Believe!	Stanleytown

➤ To order any of these titles, please call
   800-245-5082 or visit **www.freep.com/bookstore**

➤ To subscribe to the Free Press, call 800-395-3300.

➤ Visit "Potraits of War" online at
   freep.com/news/portraitsofwar/index.htm

Portraits of War
ISBN 0-937247-42-1
$19.95

THE PORTRAITS OF WAR TEAM

Richard Johnson, artist
Jeff Seidel, writer
Steve Dorsey, designer
Tina Croley, editor
Holly Griffin, copy editor
Karen Joseph, copy editor
Patty Schroth, copy editor
Kathryn Trudeau, photo technician
Dave Robinson, project coordinator

Special thanks:
Detroit Free Press
Heath J Meriwether, publisher
Carole Leigh Hutton, executive editor
Thom Fladung, managing editor
Dale Parry, deputy managing editor
John Fleming, deputy graphics director
A.J. Hartley, newsroom technology director
Shirley Wilson Ingraham, systems editor
Stephen Mounteer, systems editor

Knight Ridder
Clark Hoyt, Washington editor
John Walcott, Washington bureau chief
Joseph Galloway, senior military correspondent

Howard Brodie, veteran combat artist

June 18, 2003

INTRODUCTION

'We knew it was the right thing to do'

Before Matthew Brady brought his huge camera and glass plates to those early Civil War battlefields and changed forever how we see war and warriors, artists captured with paper, pencils and brushes the terrible reality of man's most inhumane and inhuman endeavor.

Even after Brady's Photographic Corps captured forever the carnage of Antietam and Gettysburg, brave artists still traveled to the front lines, and they went there for a very good reason. Artists have different eyes. They see into the hearts and souls of the people whose images they draw.

I met my first combat sketch artist marching into battle with the Marines in South Vietnam in 1965. I was 23 years old. He was well into his 40s. His name was Howard Brodie. It was incomprehensible to me that someone "so old" was out there in the 110-degree heat, humping the dry hills and the wet rice paddies, risking his own life to draw his little pictures.

Years later, I looked over Brodie's drawings, from Vietnam but also from French Indochina and Korea and from the European front during World War II. How fresh they seemed. How vivid. How real were the faces he captured amid so much death and dying.

When the editors at the Detroit Free Press presented their idea of sending a sketch artist and a reporter to embed with the U.S. troops fighting the first big war of the 21st Century, the editors at Knight Ridder's Washington bureau and I were instant supporters. We knew it was the right thing to do. We knew it would give Knight Ridder's war coverage something special, something different, something invaluable.

In my first conversation with Richard Johnson, the young Scots-born artist who proposed the assignment, I told him he had to go see my friend Howard Brodie, now well into his 80s and living quietly on a ranch in the hills of central California.

The two met and talked for hours. Brodie told Johnson that he must search for and focus on the humanity before his eyes. In proximity to death, the old veteran told the rookie, there is clarity.

So Richard and Free Press reporter Jeff Seidel went to work capturing the faces and stories of the young men and women who went to war. Richard's first drawings, miraculously delivered by satellite, produced the same excitement that I had felt the first time I saw Howard Brodie's searing images in Yank magazine.

The tradition of Howard Brodie and Bill Mauldin, and of Winslow Homer's stunning Civil War art for Harper's Weekly, is alive and well and safe in the drawings of Richard Johnson and the words of Jeff Seidel. From an aircraft carrier in the Persian Gulf to the sand-choked camps in the Kuwaiti desert to a Marine column clanking and crunching north toward Baghdad, Richard and Jeff used their eyes, their hands, their ears, their art to portray the faces of war, American and Iraqi.

If you want to know the real value of that art, ask the husbands and wives, mothers and fathers, sons and daughters of the men and women whose faces, hearts and souls Richard and Jeff captured. And ask yourself, as you look at their work, if you now see the face of war and the faces of warriors in a new light.

– **JOSEPH L. GALLOWAY**
Senior military correspondent, Knight Ridder
and author of "We Were Soldiers Once ... and Young"

Jan. 20, 2003

'I not only congratulate you,
but also the young writer who
shared your experience and
did so well. You both were
sensitive and caring —
the real touchstones of life.'

– HOWARD BRODIE
*Veteran combat artist who covered World War II,
the French Indochina War, the Korean War
and the Vietnam War*

PREFACE

A short and controversial war

PRECISION-GUIDED BOMBS AND MISSILES smacked into a complex just north of where the Tigris River first bends through Baghdad, just after dark on March 19, 2003.

Gulf War II, as many would call it, had begun.

The targets that first night were Iraqi President Saddam Hussein and his sons, Uday and Qusay, said to be meeting in a bunker. A 48-hour deadline for the trio to flee, issued by President George W. Bush, had passed.

For months, and with much trepidation, the world had anticipated this moment.

That war would erupt between a U.S.-led coalition and Iraq seemed in little doubt. The United States had adopted during the Clinton administration a policy of regime change in Iraq. And many international experts said the political climate following the Sept. 11, 2001, attacks gave U.S. leaders impetus to more fervently examine Iraq's role in a world fearful of terrorism and illegal weapons.

More than a year before the war began, with Americans still immersed in the search for Osama bin Laden, the man blamed as the mastermind of the Sept. 11 attacks, Bush labeled Iraq, Iran and North Korea an axis of evil.

In June 2002, Bush told graduating cadets at West Point that U.S. foreign policy was evolving: The country would not wait until a rogue nation or terror cells from foreign hideouts attacked American interests. The country would deliver preemptive strikes, using the formidable military of the most powerful nation in history, to eliminate threats to the United States. Iraq was in the crosshairs.

The United States and Britain told the world they were convinced Hussein and his regime had chemical and biological weapons of mass destruction and were developing nuclear arms, too. The regime had to go so the politically volatile region around Iraq could be secure and terror organizations could not obtain the feared weapons.

As it turned out, planning for the war, ultimately moving 300,000 troops and equipment to the region, arguing for a United Nations Security Council reso-

lution to use force, cajoling allies, deflecting criticism – all the diplomatic posturing – lasted much longer than the actual war, which was over in a month.

On March 19, from Muslim capitals to bistros and bars in Western cities to American living rooms, televisions were tuned to the Arab station Al-Jazeera and U.S. networks to watch the war begin.

Two days later, led by the U.S. 3rd Infantry Division, thousands of U.S. and British troops poured over the border from Kuwait and raced in tanks cruising at 35 miles per hour north to Baghdad, securing towns en route.

The battles were over quickly, with U.S. victory rarely in doubt. Iraqi resistance was at first more pronounced than expected, with a cohort of paramilitary fighters called Saddam's Fedayeen, or Saddam's Men of Sacrifice, dressed in civilian clothes, conducting hit-and-run assaults on U.S. troops. There were U.S. casualties, and U.S. troops taken prisoner.

Still, U.S. troops moving unheeded under Iraqi skies controlled by U.S. aircraft reached Baghdad's outskirts in less than three weeks. On April 9, with a tug from a U.S. Marine tank, a statue of Hussein near Baghdad's center was pulled down; the bulk of combat had symbolically ended. Soon, U.S. troops held as prisoners of war were found and freed.

As spring 2003 waned, evidence of Hussein's hoard of illegal weapons eluded U.S. troops. Sporadic attacks mostly in Hussein strongholds took the lives of more than 50 patrolling U.S. troops. American overseers were trying to bring together political and religious factions to form a civilian government.

Through the first 12 weeks of U.S. presence in Iraq, 182 U.S. troops and 36 British troops died in Iraq, either from combat, accidents or friendly fire incidents. Iraqi civilian casualty figures could not be accurately determined. An Associated Press count in mid-June recorded 3,240 civilian casualties, 1,896 of those in Baghdad. Iraqi military casualties could not be determined.

– PETER GAVRILOVICH
Deputy Nation/World editor, Detroit Free Press

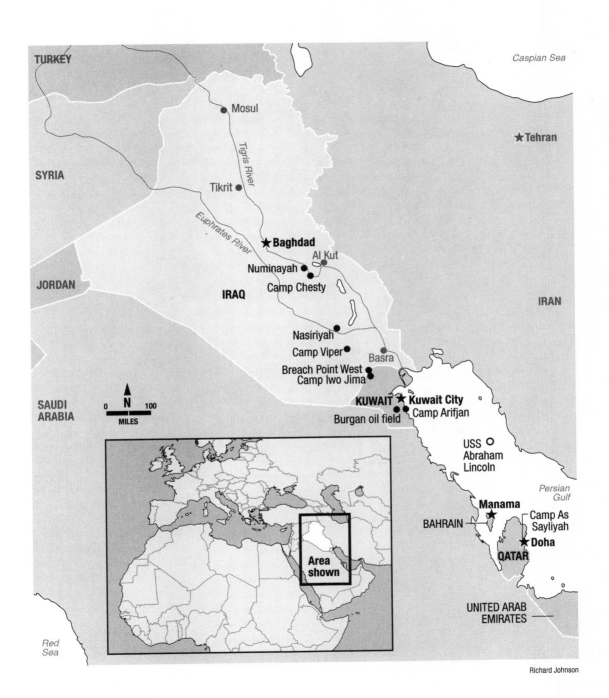

TURKEY

Caspian Sea

Mosul

SYRIA

★Tehran

Tikrit

Tigris River

Euphrates River

JORDAN

★**Baghdad**

Al Kut

Numinayah

IRAN

Camp Chesty

IRAQ

Nasiriyah
Camp Viper

Basra

Breach Point West
Camp Iwo Jima

SAUDI
ARABIA

N   100
0
MILES

KUWAIT ★**Kuwait City**
Camp Arifjan

Burgan oil field

USS O
Abraham
Lincoln

Persian
Gulf

Manama

Camp As
Sayliyah

BAHRAIN

★

★**Doha**

QATAR

UNITED ARAB
EMIRATES

Area
shown

Red
Sea

Richard Johnson

April 11, 2003

CONTENTS

Feb. 25, 2003

CHAPTER 1

Central Command: 'This is a different kind of war.'

Feb. 11, 2003

NAME: Jeffry Prokosch
RANK: Army private 1st class
AGE: 25
HOMETOWN: Sanford, Fla.
DUTY: Awaiting assignment, Bravo Company,
2nd Battalion, 124th Infantry Division

Jet-lagged soldier ponders what's next

DOHA, Qatar — Just off the plane.

His uniform doesn't quite fit.

And his body clock is all messed up, eight or nine time zones off normal; he's not sure anymore.

And his eyes are glazed from a flight that seemed to last all weekend.

Pfc. Jeffry Prokosch stands in the hot sunshine on some base in some country that seems to have only one color. Everything, in every direction, is washed in a dull yellow: the buildings, the uniforms, the sand, the horizon.

Soon, he could be fighting in a war in Iraq.

"I haven't gotten my special orders," says Prokosch, 25, of Sanford, Fla., a member of the Florida Army National Guard. He is assigned to Bravo Company, 2nd Battalion, 124th Infantry Division. He waits at Camp As Sayliyah, headquarters of U.S. forces if there is a war against Iraq.

"I'm not freaked out yet. I haven't seen anything to really rattle me yet."

But his eyes tell a different story.

Back home, he restores cars.

Back home, he likes to make music.

DJ Strange they call him.

But here? He doesn't even know what day it is.

"I left on a Saturday," he says. "I showed up here on a Monday morning, which was Sunday back home; I guess that was yesterday."

He speaks with a soft, wavering voice, almost a whisper.

Just off the plane.

Squinting in the bright sunshine.

Waiting to get on a bus.

Feb. 11, 2003

Feb. 25, 2003

NAME: Tom Bright
RANK: Marine colonel
AGE: 45
HOMETOWN: Tampa, Fla.
DUTY: Runs the Joint Operations Center
in Doha, Qatar, Central Command

Military chief finds calm in the storm

DOHA, Qatar — Col. Tom Bright packs his suitcase to go to war. He looks at his 3-year-old son, Thomas, who loves Hot Wheels.

"Thomas, give me a car so I can take it with me," Bright says.

Thomas, the terror of their house in Tampa, Fla., brings a whole handful. His dad starts to put them into his suitcase.

"You can't take those!" Thomas says.

"Then give me something I can take," Bright says.

Thomas comes back with a little silver plastic coin.

"Here," Thomas says. "You can take that with you."

Bright keeps the little plastic coin on his night-stand at Camp As Sayliyah, where the U.S. Central Command has established its forward headquarters in preparation for a possible war in Iraq.

Occasionally, when he needs to feel closer to home, he pops the coin into his right front pocket and carries it with him into the top-secret Joint Operations Center, the camp's nerve center for all military intelligence and operations, where Bright is the chief of operations.

Colleagues say the 45-year-old Marine with the subtle Texas drawl has a great "brain-housing group," a Marine term for intellect. He is praised for his leadership and decision making, for remaining calm and focused during a crisis.

If there is a war, Bright will have one of the most important roles in it.

"My job is an orchestrator," he says. "I just have to orchestrate all this expertise that is in front of me, and they help solve any problems. It's my job to make sure it's focused down a narrow road."

It's easier for Bright to describe his job in terms of past missions, instead of talking about Iraq.

"During Afghanistan, in the early days, before we actually started shooting, we were in the process of inserting special operations teams," Bright says. "During one of those insertions, we lost a helicopter."

After the helicopter crashed, Bright coordinated the security and recovery by huddling with officers in the Joint Operations Center with different specialties, starting with the ground desk.

"Ground, I need you to work with the land component to ensure we've got enough security there. If we don't have enough security there, let me know," he said. "Let's get a unit identified that can go in there."

He turned to the air desk.

"Air desk? What are we doing about a medevac procedure? What do we have overhead in the event they get into trouble and need to call in air to keep the enemy at bay?"

The people at the desks know what to do, without being told, although they often huddle with Bright to coordinate intelligence and activity from different branches.

"They are all professionals, dedicated and committed to the mission," Bright says. "All of them are dependable. All of them are absolutely tremendous. It's phenomenal how good they are."

Since the Sept. 11, 2001, attacks on the Pentagon and the World Trade Center, Bright has worked almost nonstop, taking only one five-day vacation. Bright loves being outside, mountain biking or running. He wishes he had more time to work out in Doha.

If there is a war, he'll probably get about four hours of sleep a day.

Bright has been married for 20 years to Denise Bright, a pilot for Continental Airlines.

"Since November of 2001, she took a leave of absence, which has been a blessing in disguise," Bright says. "She handles it like a trooper. Being gone is real tough on the families, especially on the wives or spouses. They do run the household while you're gone. Denise is exceptionally good at it."

Fedb. 25, 2003

Bright was raised in Muenster, Texas, north of Ft. Worth. "It's a German town, about 1,500 people, a mile square, and it hasn't gotten any bigger since I was there."

Bright's father, David Bright, spent 27 years in the Air Force. He retired in 1967 as a lieutenant colonel after service during World War II, Korea and Vietnam. He worked 20 years as a hospital administrator and served as Muenster's mayor, too. He still lives in Muenster.

"In my life, I have never met another man that comes close to his ability to lead," Tom Bright says of his father. "He is, as Aristotle would describe, a 'magnanimous man,' and I love him.

"He absolutely taught me the capacity to solve problems," Bright says. "I think the job I'm in today is a problem-solving position. No two days are the same. You are constantly focusing on a wide spectrum of issues that go from Washington, D.C., to the riflemen in the field. You are pulling that stuff together and formulating guidance and recommended decisions for the commander."

Being away from home is especially difficult on Bright's older son, Nick, 15.

"Here's a young kid who has gone from middle school to high school," Bright says. "He has a million questions about life. He and I correspond a lot by e-mail. I've taken the time to tell him stories about my life when I was his age.

"I told him, 'I'm not expecting you to come back and say anything, I just want to share with you some of my life stories because it's important.'"

Fedb. 25, 2003

NAME: Joshua Rushing
RANK: Marine lieutenant
AGE: 30
HOMETOWN: Lewisville, Texas
DUTY: Public affairs officer, also surfs
Web chat rooms for Central Command

Laptop is a weapon in this war of words

DOHA, Qatar — Lt. Joshua Rushing sits at a laptop, fighting a cyberwar. For four hours every night, Rushing surfs the Internet, trying to find chat rooms where people debate whether the United States should go to war against Iraq.

"This is a first for the military," Rushing says. "This is a different kind of war."

Commanders told him to get on the Internet to give them a chance to get their message out.

Wearing tan military fatigues, sipping coffee and listening to singer Norah Jones on a pair of headphones, Rushing scans a National Public Radio Web site and finds a recent posting.

"After America's best troops have put their life on the line to 'free' Shi'ite Muslim fundamentalists, the U.S. military will have to stay 20 years or more to keep terrorists from taking over the country that we opened up to them. Isn't there better things that Americans could be doing for the world?"

Signed "jay-h."

"Jay-h, thanks for engaging," Rushing writes back, sitting in a quiet room at Camp As Sayliyah, where U.S. commanders would run the war. "This is important stuff. As to your comment: 1. it would not just free up Shi'ites. It would liberate all Iraqi people — Shi'ite, Sunni, Kurds, Christians, etc. 2. America's best troops already put their lives on the line every day in Iraq. It's called Operation Southern Watch, protecting the Shi'ites from the wrath of Saddam's military below the 33rd parallel, and Operation Provide Comfort, protecting the Kurds above the 36th parallel."

Rushing signs the message "centcomsprsn."

Rushing takes a sip of coffee. He clicks from site to site, visiting chat rooms of some of the largest media outlets in the world. He also goes on Oprah.com and MTV.com.

Rushing decides what sites he visits and what he writes.

"I never say, 'Let's go to war,'" he says. "I want the diplomatic process to work. I just want to keep the argument in the middle, where the facts are."

Al-Jazeera, a 24-hour Arabic-language news network in Qatar, is starting an English-language Web site chat room next month, Rushing says, and he'll be one of its first guests.

Rushing is a small part of the military's aggressive public relations offensive, which includes calling radio stations, booking officers on television and allowing more than 500 journalists to be assigned to troop units.

Rushing started working by himself, but an Air Force captain was recently added to the project. Rushing wants to expand into chain e-mails.

"I can't do a lot of the live chat, back and forth where it's really interactive, because of some satellite connection problem with the States where we time out on the connection," he says.

Rushing worked in Hollywood as a motion picture and TV liaison officer for the Marines before he was brought to Central Command as a public affairs officer.

His office handled movies such as "The Sum of All Fears" and TV shows such as "JAG."

Rushing plans to leave the Marines in two or three years, and then get into acting. He's already worked in commercials.

When he's in uniform, Rushing is energetic and intense, but it's all an act.

"I'm not a type-A personality," he says. "I turn the switch on and off."

He is married to Paige Rushing and has a son from a prior marriage, Joshua Luke Rushing, 10, named for the character in the film "Cool Hand Luke."

His job is surreal, Rushing says.

"I can't imagine what I'll be telling my grandkids what I did in the war; it's going to be different."

Feb. 10, 2003

NAME: Frank Thayer
RANK: Army private 1st class
AGE: 26
HOMETOWN: Blacksburg, S.C.
DUTY: Military policeman, Central Command

For private, service is a family affair

DOHA, Qatar — Pfc. Frank Thayer stands in a Humvee, staring at the main gate inside Camp As Sayliyah, his hands on an M249 light machine gun that can fire up to 1,000 rounds a minute.

Sweat trickles down his back, and his face is sunburned, sore to the touch.

If the United States goes to war in Iraq, this is where Gen. Tommy Franks, the head of the U.S. Central Command, will run the operation.

Security is crucial, and it's a job Thayer takes with unblinking seriousness.

"This is the main gate, and you've got to be ready," he says.

There is a constant flow of workers through the gates. Local construction workers are searched and questioned. The continuous movement of people, cars and trucks adds to the sense of drama.

"I scan the area and think of scenarios — what might happen and what we would do," Thayer says. "But, sometimes, you catch yourself thinking about home or whatever. I miss my wife and family."

Thayer, 26, of Blacksburg, S.C., married Joy Collins in October, a month before he left for Qatar. "We were supposed to get married in December, but I thought it was best to do it now, just in case something happens," Thayer says. "We had a semi-big wedding. She has a lot of sisters, and they threw it together quickly."

He's six hours into a shift that started at 4 a.m., and he doesn't know when he'll get off.

"It just depends," he says. "There's really no set time. I rotate with another sentry, and she's up front."

Besides, he's used to being on a military base.

"I'm an Army brat," Thayer says. "It's in my blood."

Thayer was born at Ft. Jackson, S.C., and grew up on 12 bases around the world. His father, retired Col. Frank Thayer, was a Green Beret who served in

Feb. 10, 2003

the Vietnam and Persian Gulf wars. His brother Dean Thayer, a major in the 118th Infantry Regiment, is based at Ft. Stewart, Ga. Another brother, Capt. Danny Thayer, 34, is stationed somewhere in the Middle East with the 3rd Infantry Division.

"I don't know where my brother Danny is," Thayer says. "I think he's in Kuwait, but I'm not sure."

Thayer worked as a firefighter and emergency medical technician for six years in Blacksburg before joining the Army in 2000. "I was working at the fire department and decided I wanted a change," Thayer says. "I like helping people. That's my thing, I guess. I think everybody should serve their country."

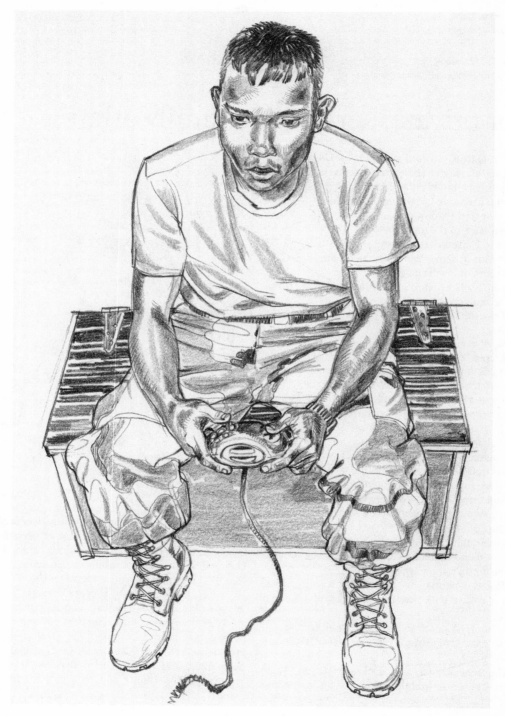

Feb. 11, 2003

NAME: Chuan Tinh
RANK: Army specialist
AGE: 22
HOMETOWN: Ft. Worth, Texas
DUTY: Mechanic, Central Command

Games are distraction from war that looms

DOHA, Qatar — After spending the morning fixing a Humvee, Spec. Chuan Tinh takes a break. He ducks into a metal storage container, sits on a battered footlocker and turns on an Xbox video-game machine.

Holding a joystick, he leans toward a small color television and begins to play Halo, an action-packed sci-fi combat game that features semiautomatic pistols, tanks and hovercraft.

"I like the blood and shooting," says Tinh, still wearing green Army fatigues. "And I like how it's not real."

He pauses, taking a long breath and shaking his head as if to reassure himself: "It's not real."

Xbox is the rage among some young soldiers at Camp As Sayliyah in Qatar, where U.S. commanders have set up headquarters in case of war in Iraq.

"I don't play the games; my soldiers do," says Sgt. Heriberto Perez, who supervises Tinh. "When they get their break times, I let them go ahead and play the games. Let them have fun. It takes their minds off things for just a moment. That's why I let them have the opportunity. It's a stressful time right now."

Tinh sets the game on its highest level. He works the joystick with his thumbs, pushing buttons, slightly jerking his body as he tries to avoid explosions on the screen. "I'm just trying to find a way out," he says, maneuvering a soldier through a maze of hallways.

Tinh bought the entire system at the base store for about $400. He plays during lunchtime and after work. He moves the system to his tent at night, so he can keep playing with his tent mates.

"Everybody in the tent area is getting hooked on it," Tinh says. "You play as a team or individual. You go around killing other people or capture the flag or play king of the hill. You go to their base and capture their flag, then bring it back to your base and score points."

Tinh was born in Thailand and moved to the Philippines as a toddler. His family moved to Ft. Worth when he was 3 or 4.

"They told me the war was going on, and they wanted to get away," he says.

He became a U.S. citizen six years ago. "I joined the Army for two reasons: I didn't like school, and I wanted to travel," he says.

Tinh decided to become a mechanic so he could learn a skill that he could use in life. He's a light-wheel mechanic, working mostly on Humvees.

"These Humvees are simple to work on, but they need a lot of attention," he says. "At any minute, any part will go bad, like lights or control box. Basically, it's simple stuff."

As the game ends, he turns off the machine. He steps into the bright sunshine and goes back to work.

Less than a mile away, inside a top-secret building in a compound guarded by heavily armed military police, preparations for the real war continue.

SOLDIER PLAYING X-BOX

Army specialist Chuan Tinh plays Xbox.

Feb. 11, 2003

Feb. 10, 2003

NAME: Andrew Lynch
RANK: Marine gunnery sergeant
AGE: 39
HOMETOWN: Tampa, Fla.
DUTY: Operations/logistics, Central Command

Can-do man can't cut the lights

DOHA, Qatar — In a windowless warehouse in the desert, inside a white, air-conditioned tent that can sleep 80 men, Gunnery Sgt. Andrew Lynch wakes up, and he can't tell whether it's day or night.

In the tent, there is a constant amber glow from lights hanging from the warehouse ceiling, leaving a dark, gloomy mood. It's the middle of the day, but the unearthly hue never changes in the tents at Camp As Sayliyah, which will be U.S. headquarters if the United States goes to war in Iraq.

"It's like we are living inside a spaceship or on Krypton," says Lynch, 39, of Tampa, Fla. "Other than that, it's not bad. It could be a lot worse. It could be raining and miserable. I mean, we are in an air-conditioned tent inside a building. How hard is that?"

Female troops live in a tent on the other side of the warehouse.

"Lynch has a cold and snored all night," a tent mate complains. "The guy sleeps in the middle of the tent and drives everybody crazy."

"I admit it," Lynch says. "I snore. Sometimes, I wake myself up snoring. I have weird dreams, and I'll be jerking all around."

He lowers his voice after remembering that a couple of men are still sleeping. On this 24-hour base, somebody is always sleeping.

There are two classes of quarters at Camp As Sayliyah. Some troops live in tents, and the others in Corimec boxes, small living areas made of metal that are stacked two high inside another warehouse.

Two troops share a box that looks like a miniature mobile home. The boxes are air-conditioned and have doors, which afford some privacy. They can hold two beds, a chair and a small table.

Lynch has been in Qatar for four months. He once bunked in one of the metal boxes, but he was recently moved to a tent. As officers arrive to prepare for a possible war in Iraq, they take the better offices and quarters. It's accepted without question. It's how things work in the military.

Some of the officers have televisions and DVD players. The troops in the tents are envied if they manage to scrounge up a camp chair or a table.

There's a saying about that: "It's not stealing — just repositioning."

Lynch has been a Marine for 19 years and served in Afghanistan and Egypt. He is skilled in the art of repositioning. He prefers not to explain the tricks of the trade, which he says — with a laugh — include "everything from getting a van to a power strip."

"My main mission is operations and logistics," he continues. "I make things run in the office. I get transportation. I make problems go away."

But he hasn't been able to figure out how to make that depressing 24-hour amber glow in the tents go away.

Interior view of a Corimec trailer.

Feb. 10, 2003

Feb. 25, 2003

NAME: Mike Carter
RANK: Army major
AGE: 38
HOMETOWN: Tampa, Fla.
DUTY: Runs the Theater Missile Defense
Desk at Central Command

Deadly Detroit streets led to a purpose

DOHA, Qatar — How did he get here?

How did Maj. Mike Carter end up on the telephone, sitting between two top-secret computers, tracking Iraq's Scud missiles, in a room guarded by barbed wire?

How did he go from a rough neighborhood on the west side of Detroit, Mich., to the nerve center for military intelligence?

He's here because he saw so many people die.

Carter was 11 when he saw his first killing. Somebody went into the house across the street, near Woodward Avenue and West Grand Boulevard.

"It was a rifle," he remembers. "Someone went in and shot up the house. I was next door. About three bodies came out of that house. It was over drugs."

Next time, he was 14, sitting on his porch. He watched two guys go into a house, heard the shots, saw them walk out, get into a car and scurry away. Carter was too scared to run, too scared to move. A couple of hours later, the paramedics brought out two dead bodies.

"It was over drugs," he says. "I saw a lot of gang fights."

The temptations were constant.

"Hey, man, you want a joint?"

Carter said no and kept walking — to school, to the store, to Calvary Baptist Church.

"Hey, man, you want to make some money?"

Of course, he wanted the money. In his teens, he lived near Grand River Avenue and Schoolcraft, and he had to catch two buses every day to attend Northern High School. But he kept walking, kept saying no, just like his mother taught him.

Dessie Colbert, now 58 and still in Detroit, was a single mother, trying to raise three girls and a boy.

"She's my hero," Carter says. "She means a great deal. She's been an inspiration because of the type of person she is. There was no harshness, no screaming, yelling or beatings. She's a very calm person who had nothing but great things in mind for her children."

Carter was 15 the first time he thought he was going to die, the first time he could sense the door swinging shut. He was riding a bicycle with a friend, and they ended up in the wrong neighborhood. A gang surrounded them.

"What you doing here?" somebody asked. "Kill 'em."

The gang members grabbed a bag and went for a gun, but for some reason he can't understand to this day, someone intervened — or rather, something intervened.

"Let them go," somebody said.

That's how he got here.

"It was shock therapy," Carter says. "I saw some things at an early age that you don't want to see, but you do. It made me make some choices."

Carter joined the Junior ROTC program at Northern High School, drawn to the discipline and sense of community, needing a sense of purpose.

"That put me on the right path. I had two great instructors, both Vietnam veterans, and they could both relate to the kids. If you chose to listen to them and listen to what they said, it gave you a lot of inspiration and energy to move forward."

After graduating from Eastern Michigan University, he joined the Army and was commissioned second lieutenant in 1986.

Since then, he has risen through the ranks, bouncing through bases in Germany, Georgia, Louisiana and Texas. He did a stint at the Pentagon, working for Vice Chairman, Joint Chiefs of Staff Gen. Joseph W. Ralston, who recently retired as supreme allied commander in Europe.

"It was an awesome experience," Carter says. "You were able to see what happens at the highest levels of our government with our military."

Within the next two months, Carter is to be pro-

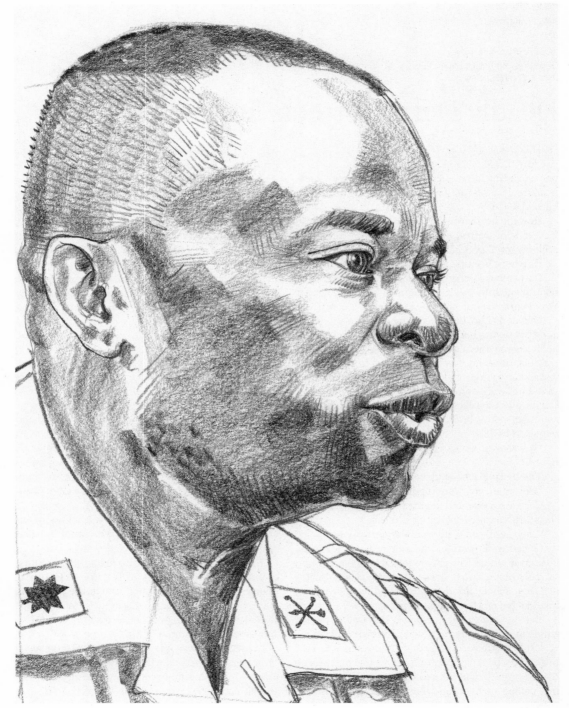

Feb. 25, 2003

moted to lieutenant colonel. Some lieutenant colonels, who later make full colonel, can become brigadier generals in about eight years.

"I was selected early for major," Carter says. "There was never an intention of coming out of college and saying, 'I'm fast-tracking. I'm going to be a general.' ... I was in the right place, right time. Good mentorship brought me a long way, and work ethic."

For the last 2½ years, he has worked in the Joint Operation Center, a top-secret room filled with computers and experts from every branch of the military. It is a long, narrow building, 60 feet by 22 feet, with brown carpeting and no windows, just a single door at one end. Down the length of the room, there are two rows of desks, pushed together into a 50-foot-long table with plastic chairs on both sides.

Thirty to 50 officers work in the JOC at any particular time, and everybody has a specialty.

Every workstation has two to four computers, at least one video screen and a phone. The stations, which sit side by side, include the Ground Desk, Air Desk and Navy Desk.

For 12 hours a day, Carter runs the Theater Missile Defense Desk. If there is a war and Iraq launches a Scud missile attack, Carter will play a major role in stopping it.

For now, it's a game of chess. If there is intelligence that Iraq has moved a Scud missile, Carter decides how to counter. Perhaps he'll make a recommendation to move a missile defense system. Or perhaps he'll wait, because some of the information that comes into the JOC is unreliable.

Carter says: "I'm just glad to be part of history. ... This is an exciting time, making decisions or making sure the right choices are made for those troops because their lives are on the line."

Carter sits at a desk at the far end of the room. On the wall, there are four large plasma televisions that can show troop movements, ship locations, real-time video and CNN. Two more screens hang above his head.

"You've got the cream of the crop on the JOC floor," Carter says. "There's no doubt about it. These guys are good. You don't see folks running with their hair on fire or banging against the walls, saying, 'I can't take it anymore.' You see folks who have been well-trained over the years."

During the 1991 Persian Gulf War, they used paper maps, pins and sticky notes in the JOC to locate troops. Now, they move icons on a computer screen.

They send information by e-mail and through top-secret Web sites, although they never mix messages with differing levels of clearance. The intelligence comes in many forms: the exact locations of ships or troops from global positioning systems to weather reports. The people in the JOC pull it all together and make recommendations to the commanders.

If Iraq launches Scud missiles, Carter is confident that U.S. forces can handle it.

"We learned lots of lessons from Desert Storm," he says.

In his spare time, Carter reads novels by John Grisham and books on military history. He carries himself with a rigid posture — head held high, shoulders back — but it's softened with a warm personality and easygoing smile.

He has been deployed for more than a month and misses being in his backyard in Tampa, Fla. — by his pool on a hot Saturday afternoon, barbecuing chicken for his wife, Angela, and their two children, Ashley, 13 and Brittany, 9.

"I miss the weekends," he says, "a quiet Saturday."

He and Angela will have been married 15 years next month. She works full time in the accounting department for a pharmaceutical company in Tampa while getting the kids to school and soccer games.

"She's got a great attitude," Carter says. "We talk every day. Some days she has good days; some days she has bad days. She's 110-percent behind me and what I'm doing over here. She's a good definition of a great military wife."

This summer, as part of his service, Carter will head the Military Science Department (ROTC) at Jackson State, as well as Mississippi Valley State University.

"I wanted to give something back," he says.

Angela is busy, getting the house ready to rent and to find a new place to live. "I start June 15 or whenever this is done," Carter says. "I'll be a professor for a year and then command a battalion."

Last month, he was selected to take command of an Army battalion in summer 2004.

"I will be a leader of a battalion that averages 500 to 550 soldiers," he says. "You have a staff and a lot of folks helping you out. It's what Army officers strive for, when they come in, to lead soldiers. I have the opportunity to do that, and I'm looking forward to it."

Why does he do it?

"I just want to be a part of something purposeful, something worthwhile," he says. "If you are 85 years old and on your deathbed, you want to look back and ask: What have you done?

"I want to lie there and say that I've accomplished something. And this is something that I can be satisfied with. I want to look back and say, 'I did my best.' "

F A18E SUPERHORNET

CHAPTER 2

USS Abraham Lincoln: 'A floating city.'

Feb. 12, 2003

NAME: Melissa Blevins
RANK: Navy petty officer, 2nd class
AGE: 25
HOMETOWN: Willingboro, N.J.
DUTY: Orders parts for aircraft, USS Abraham Lincoln

Navy mom sends love by satellite

ABOARD THE USS ABRAHAM LINCOLN — Melissa Blevins waits in the hallway, with her arms crossed, nervous and apprehensive.

"I can't wait to see my girls," she says.

Her head is filled with questions: How much have her children changed? How are they going to react? Will they be happy or sad? And how long will she get to see them this time?

"Last time, I got cut off after 30 seconds," she says.

Blevins, 25, is stationed aboard the USS Abraham Lincoln, an aircraft carrier equipped with a video-conference center, where sailors at sea can talk to relatives back home, watching each other on TV screens linked by satellite.

A few days before Thanksgiving, the last time she was eligible to make a call, Blevins started talking to her family, but the link was lost. It was a terrible tease filled with frustration, worse than actually not seeing her children at all.

Blevins is ushered into the room and sits at a table, facing two TV sets. The room is stark white, and she's wearing her work clothes: blue pants, blue top and black shoes. A camera focuses on her, sending images back home, but she doesn't even notice it.

She sees her husband, Scott Blevins, 33, and their children, Sarah, 2, and Tabitha, 1, sitting at an oval table in Norfolk, Va.

"Hi!" Melissa Blevins says, then giggles.

Scott, who is wearing a gray T-shirt, jeans and baseball cap, says, "Say hi to Mommy."

Sarah sits on a chair, dressed in a pink outfit, drawing in a coloring book.

Tabitha, who is nicknamed Sissy, sits on the table-top, swinging her legs.

Sarah can hear her mother's voice, but she doesn't know where to look.

"Sarah! Sarah!" Melissa says, leaning forward, pleading. She hasn't seen her children in person since July when the Lincoln left for a tour that was supposed to last six months. But it's been extended indefinitely, deployed in the Arabian Sea, preparing for a possible war against Iraq.

"Who is that?" Scott asks, pointing at the video screen, trying to get Sarah to look at her mother. "I had to wake them up from a nap."

The time is precious — they only get 15 minutes per call — and they are struggling to get the kids to cooperate.

Melissa giggles.

"What are you doing?" she asks.

"I'm just playing," Sarah says.

Melissa's heart races, hearing Sarah's voice. Back in July, Sarah didn't really talk much. But now, she's jabbering away.

"Are you drawing Mommy pictures?"

She nods.

"I love you!"

"I love you, Mommy."

"Will you sing your ABCs?"

Sarah turns to the television and she starts to sing the alphabet song. Melissa sings along, half a world away, never taking her eyes off her children.

They look so different, so big.

Sissy has brown hair, brown eyes and a dark complexion. Just like her father.

Sarah has blond hair, blue eyes, pale skin and chapped lips. Just like her mother.

"She has your lips," Scott says.

"I'm using Chap Stick every day," Melissa says.

The girls are running around and playing, not really paying attention to the screen. At this age, this is more for the adults than the children.

"Everything you write," Melissa says to Scott, "I can picture in my head."

He sends e-mail to her several times a day, one or two short ones, and a long narrative describing the day. They have a digital camera, and sometimes he

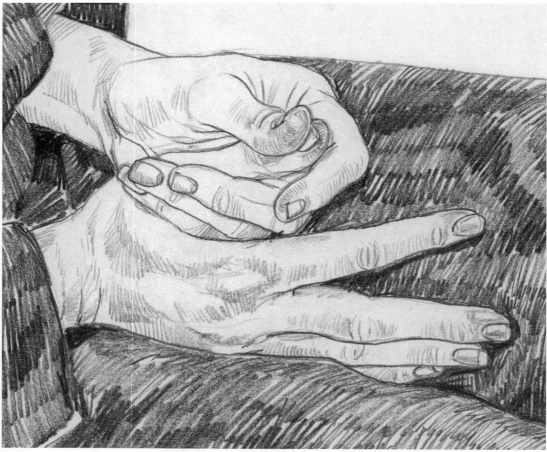

Feb. 12, 2003

includes a picture of the girls in an attachment.

But still, there's nothing like seeing them walk around and talk. Melissa is amazed at how much they've changed.

"Wow, they are so big," she says.

Scott moves around the room, getting Sarah to work on another drawing, while holding Sissy's hand.

"I'm exhausted," Melissa says. "I'm so tired."

There are more than 5,000 crew on the ship and many feel the same way. They are so worn down, so beat up from the extended travel and long workdays, not to mention the stress of being away from families, while wondering whether there will be a war against Iraq, and the fatigue is constant.

"Can you take your hair down for a second, so I can see how long it's gotten?" Scott asks.

"Yeah," she says, removing a barrette, breaking regulations but only for a few minutes.

"It looks darker," he says.

"It is a shade darker," she says. "I got some stuff. Do you like it?"

"Yeah, I do."

"Thank you."

Sissy goes out of view because the camera doesn't cover the entire room.

"Where did Sissy go?" Melissa asks.

"She is just standing there," Scott says.

Sissy used to be bowlegged and couldn't run very well. Now, Melissa notices, her daughter's legs have straightened out and she never stops moving.

"Sissy!" Melissa says. "Hey!"

The girls are laughing and screaming.

"Sissy has changed the most," Melissa says. "All her features have changed."

If Melissa took time to think about this, to ponder how much she is missing being away from home as her children grow without her, at an age when everything is so accelerated, it would rip her heart out.

And right now, she has to stay strong for the kids.

"Who's that?" Scott asks, pointing at the television.

"Mommy," Sarah says.

Scott handles them with ease, able to calm a crying child with one hand, while distracting the other without thinking.

"I love you," Melissa says.

"I love you, too," Sarah says.

Suddenly, both girls are crying and Scott puts them both on his lap, holding each one in a different arm.

"Can you tell it's nap time?" he asks.

"I know, but I love seeing them."

Since she's been on the ship, Melissa has had one overwhelming desire. She wants to lie on her couch, watch television and let the girls sit on her lap. Then, she'll get down on the floor in her pajamas and play all day long.

"You are doing such a good job with them," Melissa says. "It's so awesome. You're doing great."

Scott starts talking, but the kids are screaming.

"I can't hear you," Melissa says.

"I'm doing what I can," he says.

"No, you are doing great. I'm so proud of you."

"I'm getting ready for you to come back and give me a hand."

"Ah, you and me both."

Melissa joined the Navy seven years ago. Her grandfather, Thomas Peed Jr., was a Navy pilot, and her uncle, Thomas Peed III, was in the Navy, too.

Melissa has always loved the water. She's always been drawn to it. She reenlisted once and extended her stay another time, but that was before she met Scott and had children. Now, she's thinking about getting out. She loves what she does, working behind a desk as an aviation storekeeper, ordering, receiving and tracking parts to maintain the aircrafts, but she doesn't know how long she can handle being away from home. She's convinced it's harder for a mother to be away from her children than it is for a father.

"I really miss you," Scott says. "Life is such a roller coaster."

"You're doing fine. I love you."

Sometimes, she sits on the flight deck, staring at the water and it's the only time she can find some peace. She looks into the distance, where the ocean meets the sky, and thinks of her family. There is only one thing that keeps her sane. She clings to a deep belief that she is helping to keep her country safe. No, that's not quite it. It's smaller than that. She's keeping her children safe.

"I love you, too, honey," Scott says.

She says good-bye, gets up and walks out of the room. The girls watch her leave and start to scream.

"Mommy! Mommy!"

Melissa stands outside, in the hallway, her arms crossed, her emotions starting to bubble, unsure what to do. The door is open and she can still hear them screaming.

Melissa can't stand it. She starts to go back into the room, peeking through the doorway, one last look at the screen, wanting to say something, but then they are gone.

She sighs, holding in the tears.

"I'm so ready to go home."

Feb. 12, 2003

NAME: Larry Decandia
RANK: Navy yeoman 3rd class
AGE: 21
HOMETOWN: White Haven, Pa.
DUTY: Administrative aide, USS Abraham Lincoln

Sailor's bunk becomes a private island

ABOARD THE USS ABRAHAM LINCOLN — Larry Decandia stands at a sink in a busy community bathroom, brushing his teeth.

Skinny and pale, he wears only a pair of boxer shorts and flipflops. It doesn't bother him anymore, to stand naked in front of others. There is no chance for privacy on an aircraft carrier.

Two chains dangle from his neck: dog tags and a gold medallion of St. Christopher, a patron saint of travelers.

"My mom sent this to me about a month ago because it's her favorite saint," he says. "She says as long as I wear this, it will keep me safe and bring me back alive."

Decandia has been aboard the USS Abraham Lincoln, an aircraft carrier with more than 5,000 sailors, for all but two of the last 13 months — the length of his marriage to Jeanie Decandia.

"We were supposed to pull in on my anniversary, Jan. 19, but we ended up getting extended," Decandia says. "That was my anniversary present from the Navy."

He sleeps in a small, cramped bunk, slightly bigger than a coffin — 30 inches wide, about 6 feet long with 30 inches of headroom.

Sometimes he dreams he's running across a field of grass and he sits up and smacks his head on the bunk above.

"You get used to it," he says. "It's actually kind of cozy. This is your one true private space on the boat. You close your curtains and this is yours."

In his bunk area, he keeps only one memento from home. It's a postcard of the San Antonio River Walk.

"Hey baby," the card reads. "I miss and love you so much. Soon we'll be together again. Take care. XOXOXOXO. Your wife, Jeanie."

There are no other pictures in his living space.

"I don't want my mind to totally be back there,

Feb. 12, 2003

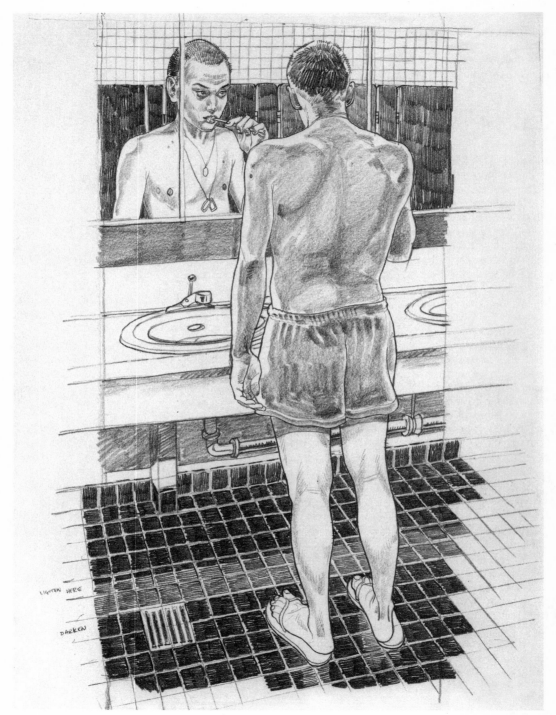

Feb. 12, 2003

because I'm not back there," says Decandia, 21. "I'm here. I've got to be ready to do what I have to do. I have to be focused. If something happens, you need all your wits about you. You can't be lost back home."

He e-mails his wife several times a day and calls her once a week. She is staying with her parents in San Antonio, Texas.

"Jeanie's father was in the Air Force for 21 years, so she's used to the life, and she has a lot of family there, so it's working out well," Decandia says.

When he learned that the Lincoln's deployment was being extended, Decandia was disappointed but not crushed.

"As much as I love my wife, I was a sailor before I met her," he says. "This is what I'm here to do."

Since the Lincoln arrived in the Persian Gulf, the weather has been steady: blue skies and sunshine.

"I really miss winter," Decandia says. "I really miss skiing."

He left behind a set of skis at his parents' home in White Haven, Pa., about 90 minutes north of Philadelphia, and he wants desperately to hit the slopes.

"The first two things my dad taught me to do were fish and ski, so I've been skiing since I was 5 years old."

Decandia joined the Navy in 1999. He wanted an adventure: "I don't like to stay in one place too long."

He works behind a desk for the ship's executive officer, or XO, shuffling paperwork and correspondence. Eventually, he wants to get a college degree and study law, but in a few months he plans to reenlist.

"I want to get back to shore and clear my head a little bit," he says, "but I think I'm going to do another four years."

More than anything, he misses Sunday mornings at home, sleeping late, going to church and then getting breakfast at a pancake house. He would hit the all-you-can-eat buffet: "They'd have bacon, french toast, scrambled eggs, fresh fruit," he says, his eyes growing wide, as if he can taste it. "I'd get a little bit of everything. Man, it doesn't get any better than that. It was a Sunday ritual for us."

He savors the memory and tries to keep a positive attitude.

"As hard as things get, you don't want to project a negative attitude. There are a lot of people aboard who came here right from boot camp. They've never been away from Mom and Dad, and they may be in a bad mood. They don't need my bad mood. We are a family. Everybody in this room, this is all we got. This is who will make or break you, life and death."

Feb. 12, 2003

NAME: JP Ratuita
RANK: Navy petty officer 2nd class
AGE: 21
HOMETOWN: Los Angeles, Calif.
DUTY: Painter, USS Abraham Lincoln

Petty officer pays attention to detail

ABOARD THE USS ABRAHAM LINCOLN — Petty Officer 2nd Class JP Ratuita stands on a milk crate, painting a star on an FA18 Hornet fighter jet.

"I view it as an art form," he says.

Ratuita, 21, works slowly, precisely, taping a border around the star, wanting it to look just right.

The Hornet is an all-weather attack jet that can double as a fighter. It is used as an escort and for close air support of ground troops. It's 56 feet long with a wingspan of 37.5 feet, but when Ratuita stands next to it, working inside the Lincoln's massive hangar bay just below the flight deck, the jet looks much smaller.

Ratuita, who's from Los Angeles, Calif., joined the Navy to pay for school.

"I miss my family, friends and home-cooked meals," he says.

The hangar bay is buzzing with activity, all day and all night. About 50 feet from Ratuita, several sailors stand at attention, wearing dress whites. They are being disciplined for breaking a ship rule.

Not far away, about 30 sailors are doing aerobics. Others are jumping rope. The Navy encourages its sailors to exercise, but only a few have time to do it.

Feb. 12, 2003

Feb. 14, 2003

NAME: David Lee
AGE: 26
RANK: Navy petty officer 3rd class
HOMETOWN: Bayside, N.Y.
DUTY: Crash and salvage crewman,
USS Abraham Lincoln

Firefighter can take the heat, bulky suit

ABOARD THE USS ABRAHAM LINCOLN —
David Lee sits and waits, hoping he never has to go
to work.

Lee is a crash and salvage crewman aboard the
USS Abraham Lincoln, which means, basically, he's
a firefighter.

"I just wanted to be in a position to save lives, in case
something happens," says Lee, 26, of Bayside, N.Y. "We
are always ready for it. If it happens, it happens."

He wears a bulky, silver fireproof suit that makes
him look like the Michelin Man wrapped in aluminum foil. It took several days for him to get used
to wearing the outfit, while baking in the sunshine
on the flight deck.

"It's been pretty cloudy the last couple of days, so
it hasn't been too bad," Lee says. "When we first
pulled into the gulf, it was really hot. Now, we are
used to it. We've been wearing it for six or seven
months straight. At first, it's really hot and annoy-
ing, but you get used to it."

Lee sits on a two-person vehicle that looks like a
golf cart converted into a mini-fire engine. It is filled
with foam and has a nozzle, similar to the ones used
by fire departments.

Like most firefighters, he spends his day waiting
for disaster.

"If an aircraft comes in with some hydraulic fail-
ure, we have to get up and do some stuff to the aircraft," he says. "But that's about it."

During his spare time, he studies or watches television.

He joined the Navy to get out of New York for a
while. However, he finds the energy and activity
around the flight deck to be similar to the Big
Apple's.

"It's always busy, always something going on, just
like New York. There are people all around, except

Feb. 14, 2003

they aren't in business suits."

After talking about home, he starts to realize
some of the things he misses.

"I miss Greek food and Mom's home-cooking,"
Lee says. "The bars. Everything that goes with the
bars: the girls, the clubs."

And he misses his 1991 BMW. He hasn't driven a
car in eight months.

"I get to drive this thing every once in a while,"
he says, patting the miniature fire truck. "But I miss
driving."

Feb. 14, 2003

Gunners keep close eye on Persian Gulf

ABOARD THE USS ABRAHAM LINCOLN —
Tamekia Dixon and Jim Avery sit side by side, alone
in their thoughts, facing the Persian Gulf, within an
arm's reach of an M60 machine gun.

To their right is another powerful gun, a .50-cal-
iber machine gun.

"I'm just trying to keep my eye out for stuff —
helicopters, planes and boats," Dixon says. "Lately,
we've been seeing a lot of jellyfish."

Dixon joined the Navy seven months ago.

"I wanted to fight for my country," she says. "After
Sept. 11, I wanted to make a difference. I wanted to
show Osama bin Laden and them that we can fight
back."

Dixon and Avery sit one level below the flight
deck of the aircraft carrier USS Abraham Lincoln.
As planes are shot into the air off a catapult, the
noise is deafening.

"I'm just doing what I can to protect the ship,"
Avery says.

He joined the Navy three years ago to travel and
pay for college.

"I want to go to college at Georgia State University in Atlanta," he says. "I want to study criminal
justice. I don't want to be a cop. I want to be behind
the scenes."

Feb. 14, 2003

NAME: Jim Avery (right)
RANK: Navy petty
officer 3rd class
AGE: 24
HOMETOWN:
Decatur, Ga.
DUTY: Operates
.50-caliber machine gun,
USS Abraham Lincoln

NAME: Tamekia Dixon (top)
RANK: Navy seaman
AGE: 18
HOMETOWN: Columbia, S.C.
DUTY: Operates
.50-caliber machine gun,
USS Abraham Lincoln

Feb. 14, 2003

Feb. 14, 2003

NAME: Brett Ernenputsch
AGE: 21
RANK: Navy aviation structural mechanic
HOMETOWN: San Diego, Calif.; lived in Ann Arbor, Mich., 1995-99
DUTY: Center deck operator, USS Abraham Lincoln

Feb. 14, 2003

On flight deck, life gets noisy

ABOARD THE USS ABRAHAM LINCOLN — Brett Ernenputsch puts his feet inside a small hole in the runway and hides behind a thick metal hatch, facing the airplane about to take off over his head.

An EA6B Prowler, a twin-engine aircraft that jams radar and radio equipment, comes screaming down the flight deck of the USS Abraham Lincoln.

The flight deck begins to tremble like an earthquake. The noise is deafening. Someday, if the world comes to an end, this is what it might feel like.

Ernenputsch coils his body, ready for the blast. His hands are covered with grease and grime. It's a dirty, filthy job, shooting airplanes off an aircraft carrier.

In a split second, the Prowler shoots over his head and soars into the air. The force knocks him over.

"You ever been in a car wreck?" Ernenputsch asks, laughing. "Every time, that's what it feels like. You feel the impact through your whole body. It's a rush."

Ernenputsch is a center deck operator, one of the strangest jobs on the aircraft carrier.

"It's my responsibility so the plane can leave this deck without going into the water," he says.

A catapult accelerates an aircraft from 0 to 180 m.p.h. in less than 3 seconds. The weight of each aircraft determines the amount of thrust provided by the catapult.

But what happens to the catapult after the plane is airborne?

Ernenputsch stops the catapult by setting up a water-braking system under the deck. He has to check the wind and the weight of the aircraft — the weights change depending on fuel and ordnance — to determine how much water pressure is needed to stop the catapult before it flies through the end of the ship.

"The cats are that fast and that heavy," he says.

Sweat trickles down his forehead. The Prowler is long gone, but Ernenputsch is left in a cloud of exhaust.

"It's really exciting at first," Ernenputsch says. "You get kind of nervous at times. After being out at sea for seven months, you get into the swing of things. But I feel really privileged to do what I do. How many other 21-year-olds do you know out in the middle of — where are we again? — oh yeah, the Persian Gulf, with all this going on, launching aircrafts and seeing the world?"

The flight deck looks like a plate of M&Ms. Hundreds of sailors work in different colored T-shirts, which signify their jobs and responsibilities. The green shirts are involved in launch and recovery, the red shirts handle ordnance, the blue and brown shirts tie down the aircraft, and the yellow shirts do the directing.

Ernenputsch is a green shirt. He wears a helmet, goggles, long-sleeved T-shirt, a dark green vest and green camouflage pants — at least, they used to be green.

"It's definitely cool," he says. "It's thrilling, always a rush."

When he's not at sea, he tries to spend as much time as possible with his wife, Katie Ernenputsch.

"We never know when we are going out to sea again," he says.

Brett and Katie were married eight months ago in Everett, Wash., where the Lincoln is based. One month later, he was gone.

"We are going to do the big wedding thing when I get home," he says. "We rushed it because I want to keep her."

Ernenputsch works about 18 hours a day.

"When I'm not working, I shower and sleep," he says. He relaxes by taking long, hot showers, even though the ship is under an order to conserve water.

Sometimes, he goes straight from the shower into his bunk.

"I bought one of those fuzzy blankets in Bahrain, so it makes my rack a little more comfortable," he says.

The Lincoln has been at sea since July.

"I miss good food, my wife, my couch and my shower — my single shower, where there aren't six other stalls. I don't have to wear sandals in showers at home. I miss drinking beer, honestly. And I miss playing hockey."

Ernenputsch was born in San Diego and lived in Ann Arbor, Mich., from 1995 to 1999.

"I just love Michigan. I love the Red Wings."

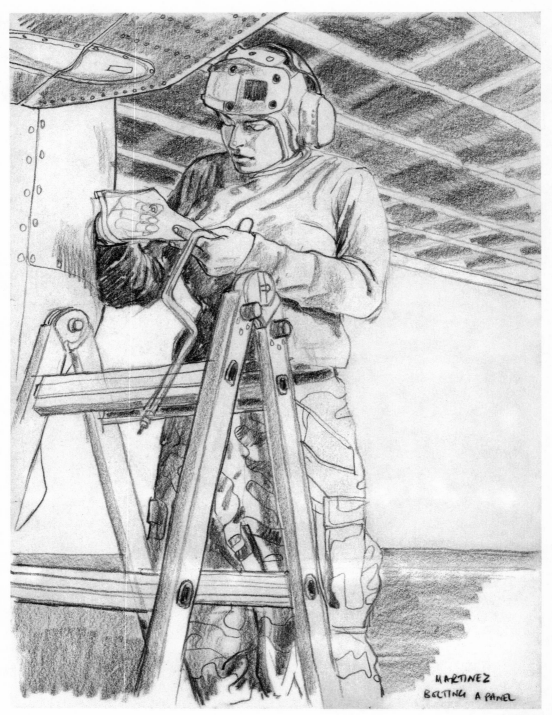

MARTINEZ
BOLTING A PANEL

Feb. 14, 2003

NAME: Angelica Martinez
RANK: Navy airman
AGE: 19
HOMETOWN: Los Angeles, Calif.
DUTY: Plane captain, USS Abraham Lincoln

Elbow grease adds shine to aircraft

ABOARD THE USS ABRAHAM LINCOLN — Standing on a ladder, Angelica Martinez sprays rubbing alcohol on the tail of an S3B Viking, an anti-submarine aircraft. She wipes it clean, like someone polishing a cherished piece of furniture that's been in the family for generations.

"After we inspect our aircraft, we make sure we clean them," Martinez says. "We make sure there isn't dust inside or corrosion."

Martinez, 19, who was born in El Salvador and raised in Guatemala, was sent to Los Angeles, Calif., when she was 13 to live with her two sisters.

"My dad wanted me to study and have a second language and have better opportunities," she says. "So he sent me to live with my sisters."

Martinez is a plane captain. "We launch the birds," she says. "We do all the signals, and we start the engines for the pilots."

She joined the Navy for the challenge.

"My friend tried to join the Navy, and he couldn't," she says. "I told him, 'You can make it. I'm going to make it.' So I went and took the test and passed the test. But I said, 'Nah, I'm not going to join.'"

Then one of her friends joined the Navy.

"She came back and told me it's not that hard; it's easy," Martinez says. "So I said, 'If she can do it, I can do it, too.'"

Martinez has been aboard the USS Abraham Lincoln since it deployed in July.

Feb. 14, 2003

Feb. 14, 2003

NAME: Richard Mynatt
RANK: Navy petty officer 1st class
AGE: 36
HOMETOWN: Phoenix, Ariz.
DUTY: Aviation machinist, USS Abraham Lincoln

He fine-tunes a superjet, but longs for his Firebird

ABOARD THE USS ABRAHAM LINCOLN —
Richard Mynatt kneels under a broken-down Super
Hornet jet, trying to figure out what's wrong.

He puts his hands inside the engine and closes his
eyes, working by touch, twisting the power trans-
mission shaft, trying to spin the blades of the engine,
but they won't budge.

Mynatt wipes sweat off his face, unable to solve
the mystery.

Why won't this bird fly?

If the United States goes to war against Iraq,
some expect the Super Hornet, the Navy's new lon-
grange strike fighter, to be the star.

Earlier in the day, this Super Hornet was on the
flight deck with its engines fired up, hooked up to the
catapult, getting ready to take off from the USS Abraham Lincoln, but the engine backfired four times.

It's Mynatt's job to figure out why. Working in the
hangar bay, he takes out a tiny camera with a hand-
held video screen and maneuvers the camera inside
the engine, looking at various parts.

Finally, he decides to replace the engine. It takes
only about 20 minutes to pop out the bad one, but he
waits to get a new one.

"It's a quick turnaround," he says. "It will be ready
to go tomorrow. When stuff like this happens, I'm
used to it. I've been doing this type of work for 16
years. Nothing really surprises me anymore."

You never know what to expect with a new jet.

This is the first deployment of a Super Hornet
aboard an aircraft carrier. The plane had its first
combat action Nov. 6, 2002. A Super Hornet from the
Lincoln fired at two Iraqi surface-to-air missile
launchers in the southern no-fly zone.

Feb. 14, 2003

By all accounts, the Super Hornet is an amazing, dependable machine. It is an upgrade of the FA18 Hornet.

"What makes the Super Hornet better than the Hornet is: this one has a larger fuel capacity and it's got two extra weapon stations," Mynatt says.

Mynatt joined the Navy in 1987. "I was going to Scottsdale Community College, and I wasn't doing very well, and I didn't want to waste any more of my parents' money," he says. "I was bored in Phoenix and wasn't sure what I was going to do. I ended up joining the Navy. It taught me a lot of discipline. It kept me out of trouble, that's for sure."

Mynatt is based in Lemoore, Calif., where the Super Hornet squadron is stationed. He is married to Pamela Mynatt and has two children, Tiffany, 18, and Kyle, 11.

He has done six western Pacific cruises, and he says they're a lot better now that the crew has access to e-mail. "Now, we talk to each other two or three times a day, just through e-mail. That makes it a lot easier, just the experience of doing this before."

Recently, he received an e-mail from his wife.

"Honey, you wouldn't believe what I did today," she wrote. "I traded in the minivan for a 2000 Firebird."

He was shocked. Then he was excited. He has always liked Pontiac Firebirds.

"Luckily, the kids are older, and we are out of the minivan syndrome," Mynatt says. "I look forward to getting home and driving that Firebird."

The man who works on jets all day plans to make the Firebird go a little faster.

"I'll juice it up a little bit."

Feb. 15, 2003

NAME: Keith Jones
RANK: Navy petty officer 1st class
AGE: 32
HOMETOWN: Bridgeton, N.J.
DUTY: Disc jockey, USS Abraham Lincoln

Navy disc jockey building an audience

ABOARD THE USS ABRAHAM LINCOLN — In a cramped radio station, Keith Jones speaks into a microphone to sailors aboard the USS Abraham Lincoln.

You expect him to scream like Robin Williams: Good morning, Persian Gulf!

But he doesn't.

Jones is calm and collected, doing a radio show that can be heard throughout the aircraft carrier every morning as more than 5,000 sailors spend an hour cleaning the ship.

Jones calls it Happy Hour!

The sailors are scrubbing stairs and washing floors.

Jones speaks in a deep, gravelly voice, reading the leadership tip of the day:

No organization is stronger than the quality of its leadership, or ever extends its constituency far beyond the degree to which its leadership is representative. Edgar Powell.

Jones, 32, of Bridgeton, N.J., about 45 miles south of Philadelphia, started this radio station in August.

"I pretty much built this radio station. I told them what I wanted," Jones says.

When the Lincoln was deployed in July, getting listeners was a challenge. "The first two months, no one listened," he says. "You thought you were just talking to yourself. We couldn't give away a CD."

The radio station runs live programming from 7:30 a.m. until almost 10 p.m. daily, using volunteer DJs.

"We have a guy who fixes airplanes," Jones says.

"Every day, from 4 to 6, he's here, Monday through Saturday."

The Lincoln has been at sea since July, one of the longest tours ever for an aircraft carrier of its size. Jones misses his wife, Barbara, and his two children, Jordan, 7, and Joshua, 2.

"And I miss Philadelphia cheese steaks," Jones says. "And I was missing Tastykakes. Those are a Philadelphia delicacy. My mom sent me a box for Christmas."

Tastykakes? Are they doughnuts?

"How dare you," he says. "Scoff at the notion."

His favorites include butterscotch krimpets with the icing on top and jelly krimpets with the jelly in the center.

More than Tastykakes, Jones misses watching the Philadelphia Eagles.

"The hardest thing about me joining the Navy was losing my season tickets," he says. "I had season tickets to the Eagles for five years. I would be at every home game. I had to sell them because I left."

Jones was on the Lincoln, following the Eagles in the playoffs, trying to catch games on radio.

They went to the NFC Championship Game, falling to Tampa Bay, 27-10.

"It will take me 20 years to get over that loss," Jones says. "Home field advantage! Against Tampa Bay! I was there the last two times they won. They kicked Tampa Bay's butt for two years in a row, and I was there. And this time, I wasn't there, and they lose."

Feb. 14, 2003

NAME: Roxy Vazquez
RANK: Navy seaman
AGE: 19
HOMETOWN: Leesburg, Fla.
DUTY: Secures aircraft, USS Abraham Lincoln

Toting chains for planes, freedom

ABOARD THE USS ABRAHAM LINCOLN — Roxy Vazquez wears the greasy chains like a shawl, loose around her shoulders, long down her back.

"There are six chains here," she says. "I'd say it's 20 or 30 pounds. They are tie-down chains. If the boat does a heavy roll, it keeps the planes tied down and they won't slide."

Vazquez, 19, is stationed aboard the USS Abraham Lincoln, an aircraft carrier with a crew of more than 5,000, somewhere in the Persian Gulf. She wears a brown shirt, brown vest and brown pants, signifying her duties on the flight deck where workers wear specific colors coded to their jobs and responsibilities.

Vazquez has an extremely physical job. As a plane lands on the flight deck, she has to carry the chains to the plane and tie the aircraft down.

"The chains aren't that heavy," she says. "Sometimes, you have to carry more. There are times when you have to carry 12 of them, and they slow you down."

The chains are greasy, so she wears rubber gloves.

Still, she says, "you have to wash your hands three or four times, just to get the chain grease to come off."

Vazquez joined the Navy 18 months ago to get out of Leesburg, Fla.

"It's a relatively small town," she says. "I needed to get away, and I didn't feel like going to school."

She worked in a grocery store, where she'd see veterans wearing old caps from Navy ships, but she didn't understand the pride. Now when she goes home, wearing her uniform, she can sense the respect.

"I have old people looking at me, and they are like, 'Wow,' " she says. "It's cool. You get a lot more respect.

Feb. 14, 2003

My friends are like, 'Wow, we never thought you'd be doing what you are doing.' "

The Lincoln has been at sea since July, and Vazquez is going stir-crazy.

"There's not much you can do on the boat but sleep, work or work out," she says.

But sleep can be hard to find on a ship.

"I sleep two decks below where they catch the planes on the wire," she says.

The planes land day and night, making an extremely loud noise as the tail hook catches one of four steel cables stretched across the deck. They arrive going 150 m.p.h. and stop within about 320 feet.

Vazquez doesn't plan to be toting chains for long. In October, she hopes to start training for the Navy military police.

NAME: Chris Starks
RANK: Navy seaman apprentice
AGE: 19
HOMETOWN: Scranton, Pa.
DUTY: Forward lookout, USS Abraham Lincoln

Navy sets teen on right course

ABOARD THE USS ABRAHAM LINCOLN — Chris Starks stands watch on forward lookout, scanning the horizon for ships and planes and bomb-toting dolphins.

He's perched 10 stories above the flight deck, more than 13 stories above the choppy waters of the Persian Gulf, looking through powerful binoculars and trying to protect an aircraft carrier with a crew of more than 5,000.

In the distance, he spots a ship.

"One of ours," he says.

Starks, 19, of Scranton, Pa., is a sailor on the USS Abraham Lincoln. He is a seaman apprentice, one rung higher than a recruit, the Navy's lowest rank.

"You gotta be on top of your game out here," he says. "You have to have great vision and sharp eyes to spot things in the distance. If the radar fails, they are depending on me. I'm the last line of defense.

"If there is a dolphin or whale in the water, we have to report it. It sounds corny, but you never know because it could be something electrical, some kind of weird bomb."

He considers it an awesome responsibility to protect the ship, and for the first time in his life he can handle it.

"The Navy has changed my life," he says. "If I wasn't doing this, I'd be in a gutter someplace."

ON SEPT. 11, 2001, Starks was switching TV channels, looking for cartoons.

"I was mad because the cartoons weren't on," he remembers.

He stopped on a channel and watched the second hijacked airplane crash into the World Trade Center. That moment changed his life. He felt anger, sadness, frustration and a rush of patriotism.

After the towers collapsed, he called a Navy

Feb. 14, 2003

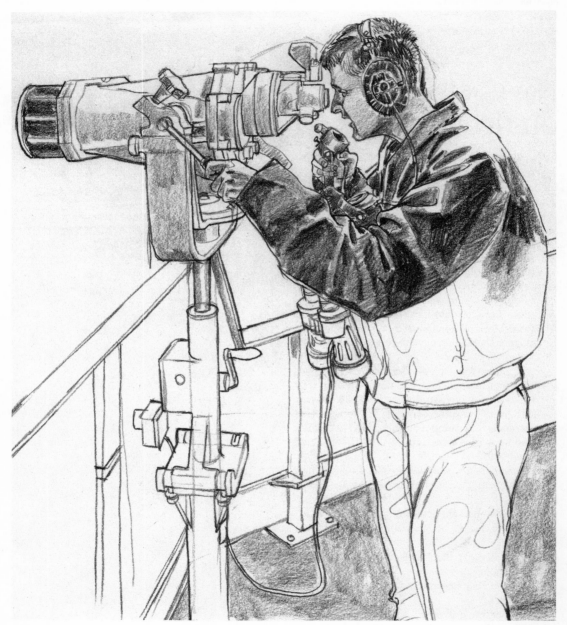

Feb. 14, 2003

recruiting office and asked whether he could join.

"Why the Navy? I wouldn't have made it through Marine boot camp," Starks says.

He was still a senior in high school but had enough credits to graduate. He enlisted, and the school superintendent allowed him to graduate early. Five months after Sept. 11, Starks was in the Navy.

"Boot camp was surprisingly easy, a lot easier than I thought it was going to be," Starks says. "I thought it would be like 'Full Metal Jacket.' I thought they would be in your face, yelling at you every 2 seconds."

He reported to the Lincoln on June 7. On July 20, the huge ship sailed and has been at sea ever since.

"It's been the time of my life," Starks says. "I've gotten a chance to do things other people can only dream of."

The Lincoln has visited San Diego, Hawaii, Japan, Hong Kong, Singapore, Australia and Bahrain.

"The coolest part was probably Australia because I didn't go out and just get drunk," he says. "I bought a camera and some film; I participated in a tour. I got to pet and feed kangaroos, which is pretty cool."

The time away has given Starks a chance to reflect on his life.

His parents split a year after he was born.

"My mom was only 15 or 16 when she had me," Starks says. "My dad was something like 18."

Starks ended up in residential treatment facilities. He described those as places "for kids who have nowhere else to go. It's not like an orphanage; it's worse. I was in five or six of 'em."

At 16, Starks moved in with his uncle, Bill Seeley, in Scranton.

"I always got in trouble, like drinking when I wasn't supposed to," Starks says. "It was your usual teenaged stuff. They'd ground me, take away the phone — standard stuff."

He knew his life was out of control. He wanted to go to college but didn't have any money.

"It was a bad situation," Starks says. "I decided to do something with my life. I made a spur-of-the-moment decision and joined the Navy."

The time away has changed him.

"I've learned work ethic and responsibility, how to be an adult," Starks says.

He experienced his first real heartbreak after leaving a girlfriend back home.

"When we got to Japan, I called her, and she was like, 'You haven't called or written in a month, so I've moved on.'"

He still keeps her picture taped to the wall above his bunk.

"Wishful thinking, I guess," he says.

There was a time when Starks wanted to get away from his family, to leave and keep on running. Now, he misses them all: "There is stuff you want to tell them: that you love them, that you miss them and are thinking about them."

Sometimes, when he talks to his mother, Shelley DeGroat, she'll say: "You've changed so much. I'm proud of you."

"Nobody in my family, except for maybe two of them, ever thought I'd do anything in my life," he says. "Ha. Now, I'm doing something. It might not be the greatest thing, but it's a step in the right direction."

He hopes to be in the Navy for the next 25 years.

"I want to be master chief petty officer in the Navy," he says, his eyes tightening with determination and resolve. "Yes!"

Feb. 14, 2003

NAME: Joe Ragonese, guitar

RANK: Chief petty officer

AGE: 41

HOMETOWN: Sacramento, Calif.

DUTY: Personnel; takes care of service records and administers exams, USS Abraham Lincoln

NAME: Richard Hawkins, bass guitar

RANK: Petty officer 1st class

AGE: 47

HOMETOWN: El Paso, Texas

DUTY: Aviation electronics technician, supervises 10 techs, USS Abraham Lincoln

NAME: Klare Ellis, drums

RANK: Petty officer 1st class

AGE: 36

HOMETOWN: Traverse City, Mich.

DUTY: Interior communications electrician, USS Abraham Lincoln

NAME: Sam D'Andrea, guitar

RANK: Petty officer 1st class

AGE: 42

HOMETOWN: Chicago, Ill.

DUTY: Personnel; takes care of pay and service records, USS Abraham Lincoln

NAME: Brett Cardwell, lead vocals

RANK: Petty officer 1st class

AGE: 36

HOMETOWN: Pond Creek, Okla.

DUTY: Aviation maintenance administration, USS Abraham Lincoln

Rock the Navy: After their duty, Man Overboard kicks out the jams

ABOARD THE USS ABRAHAM LINCOLN — The flight deck goes silent — all the planes have been put to bed for the night.

In a forgotten storage room on the fourth deck, down a tight walkway, in a cramped hollow carved between boxes and wood crates, five sailors pull out their equipment.

Four speakers. Three electric guitars. Two microphones. And a drum set.

"Come on," Sam D'Andrea says, picking up his guitar. "It's getting late. Let's play."

Klare Ellis sits behind an old drum set he bought for $300. He slaps two drumsticks together high in the air.

One. Two.

The music begins.

Brett Cardwell rolls up his sleeves, tugs at his belt, leans into the microphone and starts to sing "Take It Easy" by the Eagles.

"Well, I'm running down the road tryin' to loosen my load, I've got seven women on my mind. Four that wanna own me. Two that wanna stone me. One says she's a friend of mine. Take it easy, take it easy."

As he strains to hit the high notes, veins appear on his neck.

Richard Hawkins, a 47-year-old sailor with specks of gray in his mustache, stares at the floor strum-

Opposite: MAN OVERBOARD – Joe Ragonese, guitar, Richard Hawkins, bass guitar, Klare Ellis, drums, Sam D'Andrea, guitar, and Brett Cardwell, lead vocals.

ming a bass guitar.

Joe Ragonese, a chief petty officer, the highest-ranking sailor in the band — although rank means nothing down here — lunges forward, hunching his shoulders, grinding a cheap, old guitar he picked up at a pawnshop for a hundred bucks.

Two large fans blow hot air that smells like sawdust. The wood crates are filled with aviation supplies — O-rings and other parts that fix parts. Overhead, there are long rows of pipes and bundles of electrical wire, forming the nervous system of an aircraft carrier that is home to more than 5,000 sailors, a floating city out in the Persian Gulf.

The music pumps through speakers scattered around the small space, perhaps 5 feet wide and 15 feet long. No matter where you stand, the vibration thumps your chest. Soon, your ears will be ringing, like you're sitting too close to the stage in a smoky bar.

They call themselves Man Overboard, five old sailors with a love for classic rock 'n' roll. They get together to play three times a week for a couple of hours in one of the few areas on this ship where there are no sleeping quarters nearby.

"Well, I'm a standing on a corner in Winslow, Arizona, and such a fine sight to see. It's a girl, my Lord, in a flatbed Ford slowin' down to take a look at me."

It's been a long day aboard the USS Abraham Lincoln, planes have been coming and going for 14 hours now, patrolling the no-fly zone in Iraq and going on practice runs to prepare for war, but they've all returned safely.

Feb. 14, 2003

Petty Officer 1st Class Sam D'Andrea plays guitar in Man Overboard.

Feb. 14, 2003

When the planes are back, the mood changes dramatically on this ship. It's 9 p.m. and the sailors are starting to relax. Some are watching movies or professional wrestling. Others are playing video games or cards. And a few are already in their bunks.

Man Overboard is just starting to break a sweat.

"We may lose and we may win, though we will never be here again. So open up, I'm climbin' in, so take it easy."

They rarely play before an audience.

On this night in February, they finish the song and a reporter claps.

"Thank you," D'Andrea says into the microphone. "We'll be here until Thursday."

"A Thursday in April," Cardwell quips, and quickly adds: "Or July."

The Lincoln has been deployed for more than eight months, one of the longest tours for a Nimitz-class aircraft carrier. It was supposed to return to its home port of Everett, Wash., in January, but it's been extended indefinitely.

Veteran sailors know there is only one sure way to survive a long tour at sea: You have to find a way to pass the time and escape, to find a release.

At the far end of the room, Ellis takes off his blue work shirt and rolls up the sleeves of his white T-shirt. His skin is pale. He rolls up his pants to his knees, until they look like surfer shorts. He wears white tube socks and military-issue black boots.

Ellis, 36, was born and raised in Traverse City, Mich., in a family that believes serving in the military is an honor and a duty. All three of his brothers, a sister and a niece have served in the Navy.

"It's kind of a family thing," he says. "Dad was in the Air Force."

His father, Dale Ellis, was also a musician.

"My dad had his own big band back in the day," he says.

The Dale Ellis Orchestra played all around Michigan. Klare Ellis remembers watching "Evening at

Feb. 14, 2003

Opposite: Chief Petty Officer Joe Ragonese plays guitar.

Below: Petty Officer 1st Class Klare Ellis plays drums.

the Pops" on television and his father would quiz him on different instruments.

Klare Ellis used to sit out in the garage, in the dead of winter, and bang out notes on an old beat-up piano. Sometimes, his father would join him, showing him some boogie-woogie.

Ellis started on trumpet in fifth grade and went to percussion in 11th grade. Once he joined the Navy and he had some money, he bought a guitar and then a drum set.

When he's not playing drums, he plays classical guitar.

"It speaks many things to me," he says. "Music is communication that cannot be otherwise expressed."

Truth is, he feels intimidated by the other guys in the band. They are so talented — some of them former professionals — but he's determined to get good at it.

Once they return to port, Ellis plans to rent a building to set up a place where they can practice.

"Perhaps by then we will be good enough to call it rehearsal," he says.

He slaps the drumsticks together.

One. Two.

The music begins.

D'Andrea takes the lead, singing Jimmy Buffett's "Margaritaville."

"Strummin' my six-string. On my front porch swing. Smell those shrimp, they're beginnin' to boil. Wastin' away again in Margaritaville. Searching for my lost shaker of salt."

Ragonese, 41, takes off his blue work shirt, stripping down to a white T-shirt, revealing a big, red, ugly scab on his left arm from a smallpox vaccination he got about two weeks earlier. The scab should fall off in another week or so, and he'll be fine. He shrugs. No big deal.

Feb. 14, 2003

"I think this is the third time I've had it," he says.

He stands next to a stack of lead sheets, about a foot high, which look like wallboard. He figures they have something to do with the nuclear reactor that powers the ship, but he's not sure. He's just careful not to brush against them, afraid the lead dust will get on his hands. The other day, he accidentally sat on the lead, which happens to make the perfect seat, right in the middle of the area where the band plays, but he won't do it again.

Ragonese rocks back and forth, feeling like he's in his 20s again, when he used to play guitar in clubs around Sacramento, Calif.

"There were a lot of bad influences," he says. "I felt I needed something to draw me out of that atmosphere."

Fifteen years ago, he quit his band and joined the Navy. Now he's settled comfortably into middle age. His hair is cropped above his ears. His mustache is perfectly trimmed. And his hands have grown soft. He only plays guitar when he's at sea, and he still feels rusty.

"I'm building back my calluses," he says, looking at his fingers.

"I don't know the reason, I stayed here all season. Nothin' to show but this brand new tattoo. But it's a real beauty. A Mexican cutie. How it got here I haven't a clue."

Cardwell, 36, grew up in Pond Creek, Okla., a town, he says proudly, with 1,200 people and a single traffic light that blinks red.

"Unless you want to go to college, which I didn't, you either go to work on a farm, or learn a trade like fixing tractors, or you join the military," he says.

Cardwell signed up for the Navy, following something of a tradition in Oklahoma — "You wouldn't believe how many Okies are in the Navy!" he says — and works in aviation maintenance administration. "Basically, that means I keep records for all the aviation gear."

When he was a child, his parents thought he had a good voice and sent him across the street twice a week to take lessons from a voice instructor.

"Old Althea Butler," he says and smiles. "She did everything in Pond Creek — the voice instructor, piano teacher, a little of everything."

Cardwell played saxophone in the school band, but he never kept it up and, he's quick to point out,

he wasn't really that good at it.

But he could always hold a tune.

When he's not singing with Man Overboard, he likes to relax by sitting in a corner and reading books, but he likes singing more, just being with the guys.

"By the end of the night, I feel exuberant," he says. "I'm a little sore in the throat. My range isn't that high and we push the top of my range on some of our songs."

Ellis slaps his sticks together.

One. Two.

And the music begins again.

"Smokin' in the boys room. Smokin' in the boys room. Teacher, don't you fill me up with your rules. Everybody knows that smokin' ain't allowed in school."

D'Andrea closes his eyes and strums a Fender Stratoscaster worth about $400. He left his prized Gibson Les Paul at home in Chicago, Ill..

"I'm not bringing it out here," he says. "Last time I did, it took a real beating."

D'Andrea, 42, has been in the service for 15 years. A petty officer first class, he works in personnel.

"It's a glorified way of saying I take care of people's pay and service records," he says. "I'm one of those pencil-neck-geek types."

Except when he's behind a mike. He's all Mick Jagger — full of presence and attitude.

He started playing the guitar when he was 15. He was in a rock band for 12 years before he enlisted.

"It's what I do," he says. "It's me. I have a job, but this is a part of me that will never stop. It has to come out."

D'Andrea looks at Ragonese.

All right, a little "Mustang Sally," D'Andrea says.

"Is it B or C?" Ragonese asks.

"C."

Ellis slaps his drumsticks together.

One. Two.

"All you wanna do is just ride around, Sally (ride Sally ride). All you wanna do is just ride around, Sally (ride Sally ride)."

Hawkins is the quiet one, staring at the floor, playing his guitar so well he doesn't have to think about it. Hawkins, 47, is from El Paso, Texas. An aviation electronics technician, he's in charge of about 10 technicians.

"I work on electronics gear on the aircraft," he says. "I've been playing the guitar for 42 years. I like rock 'n' roll," he says. "But I'm a blues kind of guy. I like boogie rock. ZZ Top style."

Unlike the other guys, he keeps his shirt buttoned-up tight.

"All you wanna do is just ride around, Sally (ride Sally ride). All you wanna do is just ride around, Sally (ride Sally ride)."

The song ends and they take a break, sipping Pepsi and nonalcoholic beer.

D'Andrea says his wife just bought a new 2003 Chevrolet TrailBlazer.

"She e-mailed me pictures of it," he says.

The guys start teasing him, but he isn't mad.

"If Momma ain't happy," he says, "nobody happy."

They talk about the latest rumors. When will the war start? When will it end? When will they go home? Will the Lincoln be the first aircraft carrier to leave the region, considering it's been out the longest?

Everybody has an opinion, but nobody knows anything. They learn more about the war from watching CNN than from anything they hear on the ship.

Instead of snapping under the uncertainty, they crack jokes about having their tour extended.

"Sergio was supposed to be out of the house before I got back," D'Andrea says, joking about his wife's imaginary boyfriend. "I called my wife and said, 'Hey, keep him there. He got an extension, too. We're staying here.'"

And then the mood changes.

They talk about how much they miss their families.

Ellis misses his daughter, Rachel, who is almost 6 and lives with her mother in California.

"Kids are the only thing worth something in this world," he says. "Everything else is just stuff."

But he misses bowling.

And solitude.

And freedom.

Just being able to sleep in for two days in a row.

But he knows how important this is.

"I look at pictures from 9/11, and it gets me choked up," Ellis says. "It also gets me mad, and when I get mad, I get motivated and it becomes positive energy. So I may whine about my situation, but the truth is never far away."

The break is over, and they go back to play another song. Five sailors at sea, trying to kill time.

Ellis starts tapping his sticks.

One. Two.

The music begins.

Their faces are sweaty, their ears are ringing, the music is pounding, and for just a moment, they forget where they are.

CHAPTER 3

Preparing for Battle: 'We are ready to go.'

March 12, 2003

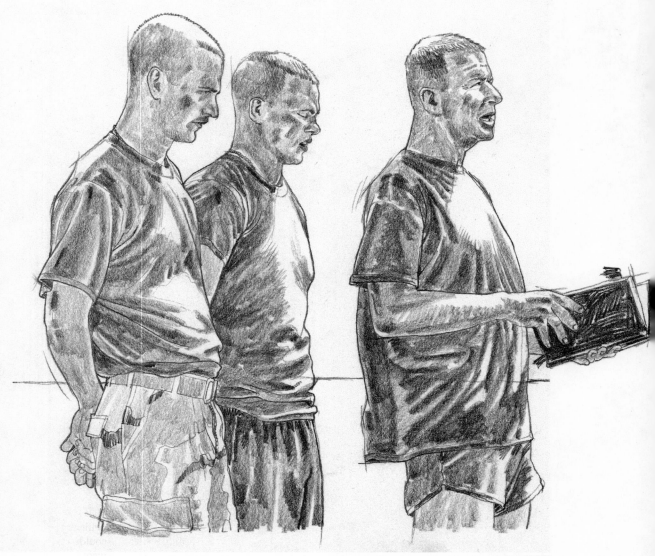

March 12, 2003

NAME: Ben Orchard
RANK: Navy lieutenant commander
AGE: 48
HOMETOWN: Idaho Falls, Idaho
DUTY: Chaplain,
6th Engineer Support Battalion

NAME: Michael Collins Jr.
RANK: Marine lance corporal
AGE: 22
HOMETOWN: Marion, Ind.
DUTY: Electrician,
6th Engineer Support Battalion

NAME: Jacob Herigstad
RANK: Marine private 1st class
AGE: 19
HOMETOWN: Camano Island, Wash.
DUTY: Bulk fuel specialist,
6th Engineer Support Battalion

Leaps of faith occupy chaplain

CAMP SOLOMON ISLANDS, Kuwait — The 16 Marines form a semicircle, wearing flak jackets and carrying gas masks. They are armed with M16 rifles and 9mm pistols, as they sing from the "Battlefield Song Book."

Lance Cpl. Michael Collins Jr. and Pfc. Jacob Herigstad set down their rifles and wait, wearing flip-flops and green T-shirts.

Chaplain Ben Orchard begins the baptism service.

"Lord, here's the water," Orchard says, standing in a back lot at Camp Solomon Islands, a base with about 1,400 Marines who make up the 6th Engineer Support Battalion. If there is a war against Iraq, this battalion will transport and store bulk fuel and water for the 1st Marine Expeditionary Force.

"We are going to baptize these men who have expressed their faith in their savior, Jesus Christ."

Orchard, a Navy chaplain, spent two years on the USS Constellation and didn't do a single baptism on the aircraft carrier.

In the desert, with everyone focused on preparing to attack Iraq, he has baptized five Marines in the past six weeks. He hopes theirs are not "foxhole conversions," a temporary religious crutch to get through the fear. He performs the ceremony in a 3,000-gallon rubber storage container the Marines call an onion skin. It's filled about 3 feet deep.

"We are not saying this water will wash their sins away," he says. "This is a dramatic reenactment of what has already happened on the inside."

Orchard has been tired, worn out from counseling Marines. Most have been here for about six weeks for what they are starting to call Operation Enduring Boredom. The conditions are spartan. While some camps have phone banks, this one doesn't. And the mail is a constant source of complaint. Some Marines haven't received a single letter.

Some of the young Marines, in particular, are homesick, lonely and afraid. When they talk to the chaplain in his tent — "My flap is always open," he says — they end up sitting on white plastic chairs, crying, searching for guidance.

Orchard tries to give each one a pep talk, but it's wearing him down. It's hard to be the strong one when you are just as tired, just as sick of the sand, just as homesick for your children. Orchard has six kids in Idaho Falls, Idaho, where he is a pastor at a church with 600 members.

ORCHARD CLIMBS INTO THE WATER, wearing green nylon running shorts and a T-shirt. The water comes up to his thighs. Collins follows, wearing a green T-shirt and camouflage pants — somebody stole his shorts.

Behind them, beyond a protective berm that circles the camp, there is nothing but sand.

"Michael Collins, one of our brothers in Christ, is here today to declare his faith," Orchard says.

Collins, 22, of Marion, Ind., has his arms crossed in front of his chest, squeezing his nose, ready to be dunked. Collins was baptized as a child, but he believes that he was too young to fully understand. He's been thinking about getting baptized for six months, and he can't explain why he's doing it now.

"Have you placed your faith and your trust and your hope in Him and Him alone, for your eternal salvation?" Orchard asks.

"Sure have," says Collins.

Orchard can relate to these young Marines. He was a hippie in the 1970s, a hard-core party guy, who wore his hair past his shoulders as a student at Idaho State University. When he joined the Navy, he was asked to detail his drug use, the specific drugs and the exact times he used them. But he couldn't remember.

"It was a lifestyle for me," he wrote.

He hit rock bottom and then became a Christian.

He felt only one calling in life: to become a pastor.

"Michael Collins, on the basis of your faith, I baptize you in the name of the Father, Son and Holy Spirit."

He dunks him backward, immersing him in the water. Collins closes his eyes and blows out a bubble of air. It's over in a matter of seconds.

Everybody claps.

"And the people said?" the chaplain prompts.

"Amen!" the Marines yell.

Collins climbs out.

HERIGSTAD CLIMBS INTO THE WATER, wearing flip-flops and shorts.

"Jake Herigstad, another brother in the Lord, another good Marine," Orchard says. "He has declared his faith in Christ."

Despite the emotional strain on many, Orchard has seen something remarkable in these Marines. Many spend their time reading or talking, thinking deeply about life, about faith.

"Jacob, do you believe that Jesus is the Christ, the son of the living God?"

"Yes, sir."

Herigstad went to church with his parents when he was growing up in Camano Island, Wash. When he got into high school, he says, he did some stupid things.

But he has found religion.

He started a Bible study group when he arrived at Camp Solomon Islands, which has evolved into a prayer group with 30 members who meet every night. They pray for each other, for their families. Three weeks ago, while singing "Amazing Grace," he realized he wanted to be baptized.

"Is your hope in Him and Him alone?"

"Yes sir."

Herigstad glances at the crowd and sees two of his bosses — Capt. Tracy Hamby and Maj. James Welling. He finds it comforting to see them as human beings, able to express their religious beliefs, not just rigid superiors who hand out orders.

"Jacob Herigstad, on the basis of your faith in Christ, as your Lord and Savior, I baptize you in the name of the Father, Son and Holy Spirit."

He dunks him.

Everybody claps.

Herigstad gets out of the water.

After the service, the Marines file past him and Collins, hugging them.

After he dries off, Collins says he feels like a new person.

"It's so much easier to come to God when you are staring death in the face," Collins says. "The hardest part of the Christian walk is to stay connected to God when you get back home."

Orchard goes for a run around the dusty camp, to release some stress. When he returns, within a matter of minutes, two more Marines are waiting to talk to him.

March 12, 2003

NAME: Kevin Greenberg
AGE: 28
RANK: Marine corporal
HOMETOWN: Crown Point, Ind.
DUTY: Truck driver, 6th Engineer Support Battalion

Marine walks proudly in his father's footsteps

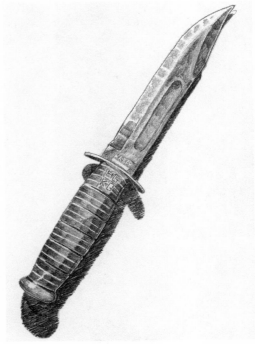

March 12, 2003

CAMP SOLOMON ISLANDS, Kuwait — The retired gunnery sergeant watched his son pack for war, wanting to go with him.

"Do you need a KA-BAR?" Richard Greenberg asked his son. It is a Marine fighting knife, with countless uses, but ultimately it is the last line of self-defense.

"Sure," Cpl. Kevin Greenberg said. "I could use one."

Richard Greenberg came back with the knife he carried in Operation Desert Storm in 1991.

He gave it to his son, standing in the kitchen in their home in Crown Point, Ind.

"You are following in my footsteps," Richard Greenberg said. "All my footsteps led home, so you come home, too."

There was almost no emotion. "My father's not like that," Kevin Greenberg says. "He's Marine Corps hard. Any other father would have had tears in his eyes. He's a gunny. I'm a corporal. He's not like that."

When Kevin Greenberg arrived in Kuwait, he sat on the back of a 2-ton truck, looking at the knife, and noticed his father's initials carved on the wooden handle.

He took out his bayonet and carved his own initials under his father's.

"It's a family thing now," he says. "But I hope to God my son doesn't have to carry it."

Kevin Greenberg is divorced, and his son, Zachary Reed, is 6.

"I took him out to breakfast the morning after we got activated," he says. "He just joined Cub Scouts. I used to tell him about the little wood car races they do. He was so excited about it. Before I left, the only thing he said to me was, 'You aren't going to be there to build my car?'

"I just started crying."

Kevin Greenberg holds the knife in the bright sunshine. It's nicked and battered, more than 20 years old, and it doesn't hold a sharp edge too long, but that hardly matters. It's the most important thing he carries. It gives him strength. If his father made it through the uncertainty and fear, he can, too.

Richard Greenberg, 51, served on a reconnaissance team in Vietnam. "He has a lot of actual hardcore combat experience," Kevin Greenberg says. "He'd tell me stories about how the other Marines would look up to him, and they would all gather around him when something went wrong."

Richard Greenberg served in the Marines from 1968 to 1972. He was in the Marine Corps Reserve from 1981 to 1993.

Kevin Greenberg has followed his father's footsteps almost exactly. After five years of active duty, he joined the reserves, an engineer support company based in Battle Creek, Mich., in the same platoon as his father.

"In Desert Storm, my dad was the platoon sergeant for the motor transport platoon," he says. "That's the same platoon I'm in now."

He has run into Marines in Kuwait who once served with his father.

"A lot of the senior staff noncommissioned officers know me because of my father," he says. "They'll recognize my name and say, 'You aren't Greenberg's kid, are you?' And I'll say, 'Yes, that's my father.' And they say, 'Gosh, I feel old now.' "

Richard Greenberg gave his son two pieces of advice.

"He told me to trust my training. And he told me to listen to my staff NCOs who have been there before me," Richard Greenberg says, referring to the noncommissioned officers.

Kevin Greenberg has always been extremely close to his father. They have the same personality, the same interests. Both are lifelong Cubs fans.

He is stationed at Camp Solomon Islands in northern Kuwait.

In many ways, his father is still with him.

"I sit here thinking, 'How am I going to do this?' " he says. "I don't know when I'm going home. I don't know if tomorrow I'll be shot at. I don't know anything, but my dad went through the same thing, and that gives me strength."

Kevin Greenberg studies the blade. "I use this for everything from opening up" meals "to cleaning my fingernails," he says. "And sometimes, I just take it out and look at it."

The other day, he wrote his father a letter.

"Every day I'm out here," he wrote, "my respect for you grows beyond my comprehension."

March 12, 2003

March 29, 2003

NAME: Yoon Ra
RANK: Marine corporal
AGE: 22
HOMETOWN: Chicago, Ill.
DUTY: Combat engineer, Charlie Company,
6th Engineer Support Battalion

He's an American, it's just not official yet

CAMP VIPER, southern Iraq — Cpl. Yoon Ra is fighting for his country, even if it's not official.

Yoon, who was born in South Korea but grew up in Chicago, Ill., is a combat engineer in southern Iraq. A citizen of South Korea, he has applied for U.S. citizenship.

"Yeah," he says with a smile. "I'm fighting for a country that I'm not a citizen of. It's not weird, because I was raised in America. The only difference between me being a citizen is the paperwork. I feel like I am an American citizen. I was basically raised here. I have no weird feelings like I'm not fighting for my country."

Yoon, 22, is a Marine reservist stationed with Charlie Company, 6th Engineer Support Battalion.

"You can join the military even if you aren't a citizen, but you can't be an officer," Yoon says. "I love working with reservists. Active-duty people put us down, saying we are weekend warriors. But I like seeing how we pull together, and we can accomplish the same mission the same way the active duty people can."

Yoon was born in Seoul, South Korea. In 1986, he moved with his family to Chicago. "There are better opportunities in the United States," he says. "My dad wanted us to get schooling here. He brought us over, me and my older sister."

Yoon joined the Marine Corps Reserve in 1999 after graduating from high school.

"At that point in my life, I didn't have any goals or focus," he says. "In Korea, every male in the family has to go into the army. My dad, Sang Ra, did serve in the Korean army. He feels every man should do service. My dad wanted me to do the ROTC and the whole officer thing. I wanted to do the enlisted side so I could ... learn how to lead."

Back home, Yoon studies animal sciences at the University of Illinois.

When he finally becomes a U.S. citizen, Yoon will have plenty of support at the swearing-in ceremony. The Marines in his squad have promised to be there.

"We are going to all dress in our blues," he says.

"The fact that I'm in the military pushes things through faster. ... When I get back, there is a fee and some more paperwork I have to send in. I'd say it will happen within two years."

Yoon could be in for a surprise. In July 2002 President George W. Bush issued an order making noncitizen troops immediately eligible for citizenship — no longer requiring three years of active service.

Cpl. Yoon Ra

March 29, 2003

March 31, 2003

NAME: Rhett Phillips
RANK: Marine sergeant
AGE: 23
HOMETOWN: Pittsfield, Ill.
DUTY: Second in charge of 13 Marines,
Charlie Company, 6th Engineer Support Battalion

Marine aspires to a career in the FBI

CAMP VIPER, southern Iraq — About an hour before getting on a bus to leave for Kuwait, Sgt. Rhett Phillips was pulled aside.

"Have you been to Marine Combat Training?"

"No," Phillips said.

Phillips, 23, of Pittsfield, Ill., had been in the Marines for nearly six years, but he never attended the course. Most Marines take it after boot camp, but Phillips is a reservist and he went to a training exercise instead. He had forgotten about it.

Phillips was ordered to stay behind at Camp Pendleton in California to take the course, as the rest of Charlie Company left for Kuwait.

"It was 23 days, and I learned nothing," Phillips says. "I basically knew everything they taught there. I didn't like it because I was with a bunch of privates and PFCs," or privates 1st class.

After he finished the class, he was afraid he would miss the war.

"I got hooked up with the rear party of 6th Engineer Support Battalion, not knowing if I would make it back to the unit," he says.

Phillips arrived in Kuwait four days before the war started. He rejoined his unit at a staging area, about 5 miles from the Iraq border.

"I kind of had to hit the ground running, but I adapt well," he says.

Sometimes, he hits the ground running with explosives. He was charging an enemy tank position with two sticks of explosives in his hand. He's not sure who gave them to him. They changed hands several times.

"I had the C4, and I didn't really know what I was going to do with it," he says. "I was going to set it on the tank."

The explosives had a 10-second fuse, and he knew he didn't have enough time to get out of harm's way.

"I knew, going up there, that I wasn't going to be able to run all the way back," Phillips says. "The tank was built in, and there was a berm on the front of it. I was going to jump on the other side of that berm.

"There was a lot of dirt between me and that tank. Afterward, it was like, 'Wow, that was a little different.' "

The tank was a decoy. And he didn't have to set off the explosives.

A few days later, Phillips got in trouble for being so close to the tank. He should have delegated the job.

"I shouldn't have been up there carrying it, apparently, is what I was told," Phillips says. "It was just a butt-chewing. It's not a big deal. Butt-chewings are a dime a dozen in the Marine Corps."

Almost nothing bothers him. Phillips is a rarity: a laid-back Marine.

"I am different," Phillips says. "I walk through life with a head on my shoulders, unlike most people. I tend to always have calmness about me, even when stuff happens. People tend to lose their head, but I told myself I wouldn't do that, never. I never do."

Phillips has a degree in criminal justice and wants to get into the FBI.

His main hobby revolves around a home theater system.

"I got huge speakers," he says. "I used to work at Circuit City, and I got a lot of stuff there. That kind of got me into it."

Phillips has a 32-inch television, but he's thinking of getting a plasma television when he returns home.

"I know when I get back home, I'll have a little chunk of change, and I'll add to my system," he says.

His older brother, Ryan Phillips, is in the Marines and stationed in Hawaii.

"My dad wasn't in the Marines," he says. "We aren't a military family. I don't know how we both ended up in the Marine Corps."

March 8, 2003

NAME: Rob Stephens
RANK: Army sergeant
AGE: 27
HOMETOWN: Woodward, Okla.
DUTY: Flight engineer of a Chinook helicopter,
F Company, 159th Aviation Battalion

Sergeant brings homey feel to helicopter

CAMP ARIFJAN, Kuwait — Sgt. Rob Stephens sleeps in a hammock, swinging in the cargo bay of a Chinook CH47 helicopter, under his lucky U.S. flag.

"I just moved out here," he says. "We call it the Boeing Hilton. It's big and dry. We always stay in here when we go into the field and don't want to put up a tent."

Stephens is planning to outfit the cargo bay with all the comforts of a college dorm room.

"I have a Crock-Pot, popcorn popper and coffee pot," he says. "It's not out here yet because I just moved in."

His laptop computer is on a bench at the back of the Chinook. The screen is cracked, but the computer works fine. It's loaded with music files. Right now, it's playing "Stand By Me."

The rest of F Company, 159th Aviation Battalion, sleeps in a tent, inside a canvas warehouse at Camp Arifjan. The company consists of 220 soldiers and 16 helicopters.

"It's a real small family from pilots to maintenance workers," he says.

Stephens, 27, a flight engineer, glances at a U.S. flag. His good-luck charm is fastened to the ceiling of the Chinook with bungee cords and string. When he's in the hammock, he can stare at the flag above him.

"This is a big casket flag," he says. "When we were in Macedonia, we wanted to fly it over the post on the Fourth of July, and I hung onto it."

This flag was with him when a Chinook he was in crashed in Kosovo.

"We were doing fast rope insertion," he says, "and we just fell out of the sky. It was one of those freak things. The nose went up too high, and we lost lift and just hit the ground. I was in a position where I should have gotten killed. I got really, really lucky. By all rights, I should be dead right now. I thought this flag is pretty good, pretty lucky, so I've held onto it."

The company has been deployed throughout Europe for about eight years.

"I've been in the Army just about nine years," Stephens says. "During that time, I've only been in the U.S. for a year and like 10 months, something crazy like that."

Stephens is based in Germany, but he doesn't have a house or an apartment.

"I have a lot of stuff," he says. "It's in storage."

His bed is a hammock.

His home is a Chinook.

Stephens is single with no children.

"I'm freshly divorced," he says, looking at his watch, "about two weeks ago."

A joke for every situation, that's Stephens.

When the Chinook is used to transport paratroopers, Stephens likes to play tricks on them before they jump out of the back.

"I tell the first guy in line, 'Oh man, you aren't going to like this at all,'" he says. "I tell them the winds are really high, and they are going in the trees. You got to laugh at them, make faces at the first guy who is going."

The Chinook is also used for high-profile visitors. F Company has transported Dallas Cowboys cheerleaders, NFL broadcaster Terry Bradshaw and country singer Toby Keith.

Several members of the company appeared in Keith's music video "Courtesy of the Red, White and Blue."

Stephens has the video saved on his laptop. As he watches it in the tent, a Chinook goes across the computer screen: "There I am," he says. "I was inside it right there."

There is one more thing they keep in the Chinook: a football.

A few years ago, they were in Macedonia and saw some kids on a hill. They dropped a football to them from the helicopter, and the kids didn't know what

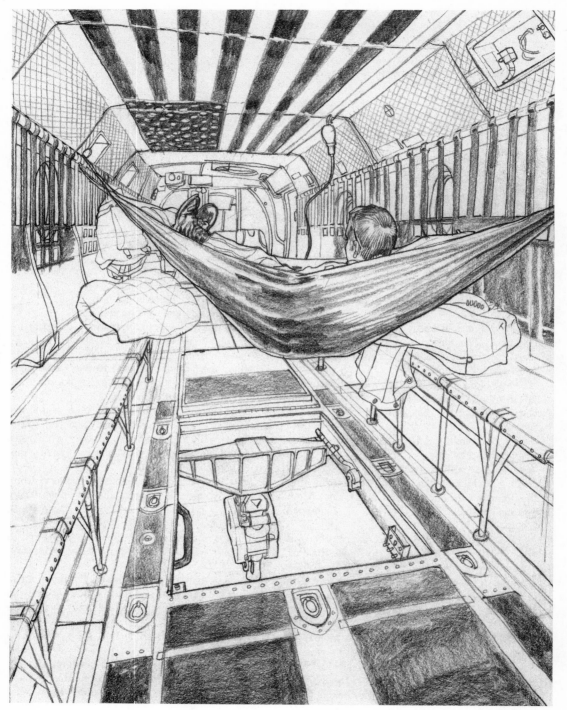

March 8, 2003

to do with it at first.

Every couple of days, the Chinook flew by the hill, and Stephens watched the kids playing with it.

"Pretty soon," he says, "there were all these little football players running around Macedonia."

Stephens grabs a football off the seat.

"It's good for the boredom. You can play football when you are flying, or we wrestle back here, whatever. You get pretty bored on these long flights.

"You can only look at so much sand and camels."

ADEKOYA
LOOKING NORTH

March 28, 2003

NAME: Paul Adekoya
RANK: Marine private 1st class
AGE: 23
HOMETOWN: Bloomington, Ill.
DUTY: Motor transport driver,
6th Engineer Support Battalion

Coffee, camaraderie keep private alert

SOUTHERN IRAQ — To stay awake on post or while driving a truck, Pfc. Paul Adekoya opens a packet of freeze-dried coffee, dumps the crystals into his mouth, takes a drink of water, swishes the mixture around and swallows it with a wince.

"It's horrible, but it works good," says Adekoya, 23, of Bloomington, Ill.

It gives him a good hour or two of alertness.

Staying awake is one of the keys to being a Marine. Almost no one involved in Operation Iraqi Freedom gets a good night's sleep. The troops are always moving or on watch.

Adekoya, a motor transport driver, has other tricks.

"I'll have a cigarette or put in a dip" of chewing tobacco, he says.

Adekoya is a junior at Illinois State University, studying computer science. He joined the Marine Corps reserves four years ago.

"I wanted a challenge — to see if I could hang with the best, to see if I had what it takes."

His parents, Deborah and Tony Adekoya, were born in Nigeria. They moved to the United States 31 years ago so they could have a better life and so their children could have a better education, Adekoya says.

When he joined the Marines, his mother cried, but his father was pleased.

"My parents had a strict upbringing in Nigeria," Adekoya says. "And my dad thought the Marines would teach me some discipline."

Adekoya drives 7-ton trucks, 5-ton trucks, Humvees and dump trucks.

"You have to drive defensive," he says.

"I have to keep my eyes open for civilians, combatants and land mines."

March 8, 2003

NAME: Susie Caballero
RANK: Army specialist
AGE: 24
HOMETOWN: Benavides, Texas
DUTY: Crane operator, 68th Corps Support Battalion

Texas rancher groomed for rigors of Army

CAMP ARIFJAN, Kuwait — Spec. Susie Caballero is on the phone talking to her mother, Alma Caballero, trying to stay upbeat and reassuring, but it's not working.

"Mom, this is my choice," Susie Caballero says. "I signed the papers."

Alma Caballero can't talk. She only cries.

Susie Caballero, 24, has always been the strong one. A wisp of a soldier, 5-foot-3 and barely 120 pounds, she grew up driving tractors on a ranch in Texas.

She's a crane operator for an Army Reserve support unit based at Camp Arifjan, about a 30-minute drive from Kuwait City.

"Be proud of me," Caballero says to her mother. "Dad would be proud of me."

Her father, Richard Caballero, who did a tour in the Air Force, died six years ago.

Caballero was 18 when she inherited her father's 2,000-acre ranch in Benavides, Texas, because her mother didn't want to run it.

She took control of everything. Back home, she handles the heavy machinery, including bulldozers and tractors, putting in a pond as her father had taught her. The ranch has horses and cattle, but it's used mainly for deer hunting. She leases it to a group of businessmen from north Texas.

"During hunting season, I'm the one who goes out and checks on the hunters," she says. "During the off-season, I fill up feeders for deer."

Caballero is a natural leader in civilian life, and it's the same in the desert.

She stands in the middle of the road stopping traffic and directing a team of workers using a 22-ton crane on a sprawling Army supply base. They're trying to move concrete barriers off a truck and into two rows around a supply building to protect it against a car bomb.

Finally, Caballero holds up her right fist. "That's good," she says.

The crane operator lowers the barrier to the ground.

Caballero takes over, jumping into the cab, working the controls and moving another barrier into place. She does it in half the time.

"It's been interesting," Caballero says. "I wouldn't change this for anything. This is the perfect time in my life to do this. I don't have kids, no husband."

Burned out from college — she was studying exercise physiology at Texas A&M but didn't finish — Caballero joined the Army Reserve in a rush of patriotism after the Sept. 11, 2001, attacks. "It's something I always wanted to do, and it was the right time."

She signed up for six years and was called to active duty Dec. 28. Her unit is based out of Corpus Christi, Texas, attached to the 68th Corps Support Battalion. This is her first tour overseas.

"My eyes hurt from the sand," she says. "My face feels horrible. I think I most miss bathing in a bathtub … that and being able to walk around in my civilians."

Her civilians? That's jeans or shorts, and cowboy boots. But she isn't complaining.

She passes time by listening to country music or working out in the gym.

"If it wasn't for my CD player, I'd go insane," she says.

Especially on the hard days, when she thinks about her mother.

After several painful phone calls, Caballero has reached a conclusion: "I want to talk to my mom, but she's taking it hard. From now on, I'm just gonna write letters."

ROPE HOLDING
CONCRETE BLOCK
TO STOP IT FROM
SWINGING

SMALLPOX
INOCULATION

March 8, 2003

Smaller

WATCHING
CRANE STABILITY
WORRIED ABOUT
TIPPING

GAS GEAR

March 8, 2003

March 12, 2003

NAME: Twila Curtis
RANK: Marine lance corporal
AGE: 27
HOMETOWN: Ft. Defiance, a Navajo reservation in Arizona
DUTY: Bulk-fuel specialist and security, 6th Engineer Support Battalion

Bulk-fuel specialist: 'No turning back'

NORTHERN KUWAIT — Lance Cpl. Twila Curtis stands watch, staring at the horizon, watching the Iraqi border.

"You have to be on alert at all times," says Curtis, a bulk-fuel specialist. "I've overcome the fear. Basically, it's from talking to other Marines. That keeps my morale up."

She is a reservist assigned to the 6th Engineer Support Battalion, which is based at Camp Solomon Islands in Kuwait. The 1,400-person battalion has built this forward staging point. There is nothing but sand between her post and the Iraqi border. If there is a war in Iraq, her battalion will supply bulk fuel and water to the 1st Marine Expeditionary Force.

Four weeks ago, there was nothing there. Now, there are protective berms, ditches, pup tents, showers, crude outhouses and other equipment.

Curtis has been here for five days, doing a security rotation. In less than 24 hours, she will return to Camp Solomon Islands.

"I have my days when I'm miserable and don't want to be here, but at the same time, I'm going to go home and be proud that I had a part in this operation," she says.

On some nights, she looks at the border, and the sky glows orange from fires in Iraq.

"When I got here, oh yes, I was nervous," Curtis says. "I didn't know what to expect. I was pretty nervous when we came out here. But I have pretty much put myself in the position where I'm ready to do this. It's something I have to do, protect myself and my fellow Marines. I'm here. There's no turning back."

Curtis, who is an American Indian, lives at Ft. Defiance, a Navajo reservation in Arizona. Her father, Andrew Watchman, 61, was a Marine.

"It was always something I wanted to do, and I wanted to be like my father," she says.

"I think he's very proud. I'm the last of my generation to be a Marine."

After spending so much time in the desert, staring at the horizon, she has had a lot of time to think. She plans to go to college to get a degree in criminal justice.

"You start to think about making some changes in your life," she says. "You realize how you take things for granted."

March 28, 2003

NAME: Brian McCoic
RANK: Marine 1st sergeant
AGE: 39
HOMETOWN: Dellwood, Wis.
DUTY: Senior enlisted man in Charlie Company,
6th Engineer Support Battalion

Sergeant leads by his example

March 28, 2003

SOUTHERN IRAQ — During a driving sandstorm, while most of the Marines are seeking shelter or walking around wearing face masks just to breathe, 1st Sgt. Brian McCoic takes off his shirt and spreads shaving cream on his face. He puts on a pair of goggles, turns his back to the wind and starts shaving.

"I have to set an example," he says. "It's challenging and miserable, but it's the same for both sides. It's hard to get equipment working, and it's hard to keep the Marines motivated."

McCoic is the senior enlisted man for Charlie Company, 6th Engineer Support Battalion.

"We are providing a lot of security," he says. "And the sand makes it hard. When you can't see, it's not a good thing. We have better weapons, but the sand takes away any advantage."

McCoic lives in Dellwood, Wis., where he is a volunteer firefighter. In Oxford, he works as a prison guard at a federal correction institution.

"It's more mental than physical," he says. "It's like being a baby-sitter for bad little children. You say 'no' a lot."

He assumed the role of first sergeant three days before Charlie Company left for Kuwait.

His job is varied. He handles personnel, discipline and administration matters.

"I'm still learning the job," he says. "I'm still trying to figure out my role in the company. I suppose it's to make sure they go and do what they are supposed to be doing. I'm trying to give the company commander an effective weapon, to keep it all organized."

McCoic, a Marine Corps reservist, did eight years of active duty. During Operation Desert Storm, he spent eight months on a ship about 50 miles east of Kuwait City in the Persian Gulf.

"We were part of the decoy that made Iraq think we were going to do an amphibious assault," he says. "We thought it was real until it started. Then, it was extremely frustrating."

McCoic has been in the Marines for 19 years. He sleeps fully dressed, wearing his boots.

"I air my feet out during the day," he says. "I can go from zero to awake pretty quickly."

McCoic has two sons from a previous marriage. Nathan, 17, was born in Okinawa, Japan, and Nicholas, 15, was born while McCoic was deployed in Norway. His second wife, Stephanie McCoic, is pregnant with their first child. She is due in July.

"I'd like to be back, or at least get leave," McCoic says, "but things would have to be pretty calm for that to happen. It's been really hard on my wife. But she's a tough woman."

When he gets homesick, McCoic says, he just works harder, trying to take his mind off things.

"It isn't comfortable, and it isn't fun," he says. "But we are doing our job."

LCP
MICHELLE
GLASS

March 28, 2003

NAME: Michelle Glass
RANK: Marine lance corporal
AGE: 20
HOMETOWN: East Peoria, Ill.
DUTY: Combat engineer, Charlie Company,
6th Engineer Support Battalion

Fighter is a Marine first, then a woman

SOUTHERN IRAQ — Michelle Glass was a party animal. She drank too much and went to school only when she felt like it.

"I was the kid your parents didn't want you to hang out with," Glass says. "When I was in high school, it was probably the hardest four years of my mom's life. I was a pain in the butt. I knew it, but I was stubborn. Nobody was going to tell me different."

Glass, 20, of East Peoria, Ill., joined the Marine Corps Reserve in February 2002.

It changed her life.

"I needed discipline, lots of it," she says. "I definitely got it. The Marine Corps changed me. It was the best thing I could have done for myself. I had to get my life together. Look at me now."

She is a combat engineer for Charlie Company, 6th Engineer Support Battalion, working security at a crucial supply base in southern Iraq.

Glass, 5 feet tall and 111 pounds, says she can do everything, physically, she's been asked to do.

"I had to prove that I'm not just a whiny girl who did it for the college money," she says. "I had to prove that I'm mentally tough. I bet a lot of guys would cry before I would."

Glass turned 19 at boot camp last year and 20 on Feb. 27, when she was in Kuwait.

"My next birthday, I'm 21," she says. "It's going to be a big party. Watch out. I have two birthdays to make up for, plus my 21st."

After boot camp, Glass graduated first in her class when she went to school to learn to be a combat engineer. She was a private first class for only one day before being promoted to lance corporal.

"I can do everything a man can do," she says. "If I can't, they need to kick me in the butt. I'm not a man, not a woman. I'm a Marine."

Glass is one of two women in Charlie Company, which includes 130 Marines. She has her own tent,

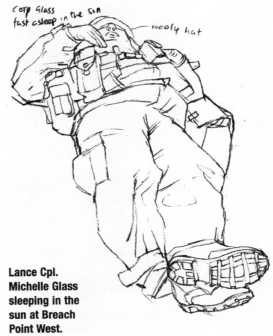

Corp Glass fast asleep in the sun

wooly hat

Lance Cpl. Michelle Glass sleeping in the sun at Breach Point West.

March 28, 2003

which is just about the only special treatment she receives. She is so accepted and praised by her superiors the guys on her truck say, "Glass? She's not a female. She's one of us."

"At home, I'm a girl," Glass says. "Out here, there's no place for femininity."

Glass has always had long blond hair down to her waist. When she was activated, she cut it to chin length, so it would be easier to handle.

On her first day in Kuwait, she shaved her head, just like all the guys in her platoon.

"I didn't look at myself for a day in the mirror," she says. "When I did look, I fit in. I looked like every-

MORNING WATCH
LANCE CORPORAL
MICHELLE GLASS

Glass on guard duty at Camp Viper.

March 28, 2003

body else."

She smiles: "But I wasn't cute at all."

Technically, she broke a rule. A woman in the Marines is not supposed to shave her head because it's considered extreme.

"It upset a female captain," Glass says.

"She was outraged by it. She told me I had to be more feminine. I said, 'There's no place in the war to be feminine.' "

The issue went to the battalion command, but there was little concern: Glass is so accepted that she was simply told not to do it again.

Traveling through Kuwait and Iraq, Glass has developed a deep appreciation for the freedoms and opportunities in the United States.

"I've never seen the world, the way people live," she says. "It's sad, so many people in America take things for granted — running water, going to the store for groceries, even having a clean place to live.

Here, these people have nothing.

"Back home, people don't know a lot about the military, don't know about the world. They don't have a clue. They don't know how other people live."

She is going to school to become a firefighter and hopes to become a fire investigator. She says she likes to figure things out.

Glass, who is single, could be called to duty for the next seven years, but she doesn't plan to reenlist.

"One day, I want to be a good wife, a good mom," she says. "I don't want to be a mom who goes to war."

Her family writes her letters, saying she might be able to find the man of her dreams among so many eligible men, but she scoffs at the notion. She used to look at Marines and think, "Dang, I could marry me one of them."

But not after living with them.

"I would never date a Marine," she says. "I'm one of them now."

Glass asleep at Breach Point West.

March 28, 2003

STAFF SGT. WADE CLARK

April 2, 2003

NAME: Jeremy Westlake
RANK: Marine staff sergeant
AGE: 28
HOMETOWN: Browning, Ill.
DUTY: Company armorer, combat engineer,
Charlie Company, 6th Engineer Support Battalion

Marine's war-zone promotion is special

SOUTHERN IRAQ — Charlie Company stands in formation, in enemy territory, in the middle of a war.

"Sergeant Westlake, front and center," 1st Sgt. Brian McCoic says.

Forty-five Marines stand at attention in the sand, in front of a ditch that is about 4 feet deep. They face three rows of white, two-person pup tents, set up in trenches.

Sgt. Jeremy Westlake walks to the front of the formation, squaring his turns. He salutes Maj. Mike McCarthy and McCoic.

McCoic reads a proclamation, promoting Westlake from sergeant to staff sergeant.

"You've been looking for this for a long time," McCarthy says, pinning the chevron on Westlake's flak jacket. During a normal promotion, the chevron would be pinned to his collar. But the Marines have been wearing biochemical suits for weeks. "I expect more out of you. I know you'll give more."

Westlake has known about his promotion for months. Still, this is special.

"To get it out here is entirely cool," Westlake says.

Westlake, 28, is a combat engineer for Charlie Company, 6th Engineer Support Battalion. He grew up in Browning, Ill., and joined the Marines as an escape.

"My town had about 300 people, and I wanted to get out of the little Podunk town," he says. "I wanted to go places, see things."

Westlake was on active duty from 1993 to 1998, deployed to Haiti in 1994, Bosnia in 1995 and Liberia in 1996.

In March 1998, he left active duty and checked into the reserves. He works full time as a corrections officer at the Jacksonville Corrections Center, a minimum-security prison near Springfield, Ill.

"I'm very happy to be back playing in the Marines again," he says.

This is his fifth overseas deployment, but it's the first time that he's been married and had a child. Westlake and his wife, Molly, have a daughter, Justice May, who will turn 3 on April 26.

"She is everything to me," Westlake says. "She's a reason not to get whacked. You don't want your little girl to grow up without a dad."

Westlake is calmer, more cautious.

"I would not be as apt to go and do hero stuff," he says. "But it would not stop me from doing what I had to do."

A couple years ago, he wouldn't think twice about picking up unexploded ordnance. "Now, if I'm not sure, we blow it up in place," he says.

When he joined Charlie Company, Westlake became the company armorer.

"I'm in charge of the upkeep on weapons, the paper trail," he says.

After getting promoted, Westlake joins several members of Charlie Company preparing to leave on a mission to blow up a decoy tank.

"I've got to earn my money," Westlake says. "What do I get after this promotion? Fifty bucks more a payday?"

March 8, 2003

NAME: Mike Steiner
RANK: Army chief warrant officer
AGE: 34
HOMETOWN: Plano, Texas
DUTY: Black Hawk helicopter pilot and instructor assigned to a medevac unit in Kuwait

BLACKHAWK MEDEVAC

March 8, 2003

Wait wears on pilot anxious for action

CAMP ARIFJAN, Kuwait — Chief Warrant Officer Mike Steiner has an impatient smile.

He's sick of waiting. Tired of training.

"We are ready to go," Steiner says, standing next to a Black Hawk helicopter.

His eyes are filled with excitement, confidence and bravado. If there is a trace of uncertainty or fear about the possibility of war in Iraq, he won't admit it.

And it certainly doesn't show.

Steiner of Plano, Texas, is a Black Hawk helicopter pilot assigned to a medevac, a medical evacuation unit, based at Camp Arifjan, about a 30-minute drive from Kuwait City.

"We've been sitting around saying this is the big show," Steiner says. "This is our Super Bowl. It's got to be what football players feel like when they are waiting around for two weeks, waiting for the big game."

Wanting it to start.

Steiner has been in Kuwait for nearly one month, getting used to flying at night in high winds and sandstorms.

"Nighttime in the desert, it's the worst conditions for flying," he says. "When you are looking through night-vision goggles, you don't have depth perception. When you are over the sand, if you get over 80 feet, you are on instruments; you can't see the ground."

Steiner has been a pilot for eight years, flying Black Hawks and Hueys, but he's never seen combat.

March 8, 2003

March 8, 2003

He's been in the medical evacuation unit for 1½ years.

If there is war, he doesn't think it will last long.

"I think it will be a repeat of the last one," he says, throwing up his arms in mock surrender. "They don't want to die any more than we do. If I were on their side, I'd be surrendering."

Steiner was 10 the first time he rode in a helicopter. His family was on vacation in Missouri when they came across a tourist stand offering helicopter rides. It probably lasted only 10 minutes, but he was hooked.

Steiner sat on the outside, looking down at the ground.

"It felt like a magic carpet ride," he remembers.

The pilot gave him a card with a picture of the helicopter and his name on it.

"I still have it in a box in a closet in my home," Steiner says.

Steiner, who is single, has flown helicopters in Egypt, Israel, Jordan, Kuwait, Saudi Arabia and the United States.

"This is the best job in the Army," Steiner says. "You get paid to go play. I always tell people that being a pilot is like when you were a kid and you'd fake being sick so you could stay home from school. The rest of the world is off doing whatever, and you are home, having a good time, doing what you want to do. That's what flying is. You get away from the bull."

March 23, 2003

NAME: Miriam Jenkins
RANK: Marine corporal
AGE: 23
HOMETOWN: Gainesville, Fla.
DUTY: Fire team leader, in charge of three
bulk-fuel specialists, 6th Engineer Support Battalion

Sisterly corporal ready to kill, if need be

NORTHERN KUWAIT — Cpl. Miriam Jenkins has convinced herself that she wants to go to war. She wants to kill somebody.

It's the only way she can prepare herself.

"You have to convince yourself that you want to kill, that you to have to kill," she says.

"You have to be able to say, 'I want to kill this guy, and I'm going to pull the trigger' and 'I just did it, and I'm going to kill the next one.' "

Her words sound jarring, coming from a person who calls herself a Southern Christian.

"I would never do it to an innocent person," she says. "If they are shooting at me, I shoot back."

Jenkins, 23, of Gainesville, Fla., is a fire team leader in charge of three bulk-fuel specialists. All are men.

"They are awesome Marines," she says. "I love them to death. They are good Marines. I have to make sure they get haircuts when they can. Make sure they have their rounds. Make sure they have their weapons. Make sure they haven't lost anything. Make sure they haven't gotten a Dear John letter. It's like I'm back being a middle sister, the one who takes care of the younger ones, but I have to answer to the older ones."

Jenkins was raised in a single-parent family with nine children. She was No. 6.

"It was just us," Jenkins says. "There was no dad. There was no steady stream of money. My mom was the poor woman with a vanful of kids, and she still picked up hitchhikers."

Sometimes, as a child, Jenkins would sleep in a bed with four others. It was a difficult life that prepared her for living with the Marines.

"Eating crappy food is no big deal," she says.

"Sleeping on the floor is no big deal. I have a cot, but I'd rather sleep on the floor. Nothing surprises me."

Early March 18, at 4 a.m. in Kuwait, she roamed around a Marine camp, trying to find somebody with a radio, so she could hear President George W. Bush give his speech about Iraq.

She found a tent with the radio playing, and she sat outside, on a wood pallet, listening to him give a 48-hour ultimatum, while watching the stars.

"It was pretty," she says. "A full moon. It was a real good scene, and it motivated me.

"I'm excited in a way. Inside, I want to go to war. This is what I signed for. This is what I've trained for. This is why I'm here. Personally, I think I'm going to be able to keep myself together."

Later that morning, as company commanders briefed the troops to prepare for war, Jenkins spoke up: "Don't worry," she said. "Bush said a bunch of motivating stuff to our parents last night. Our families back home, they know what's going on."

She feels a sense of safety because she carries a 240 Gulf.

"It's a big old machine gun," she says. "I feel safe with that, very safe. Nine out of 10 times, I'm going to mow him down before he gets that round off."

Jenkins stands 5 feet 1, and the gun comes up to her chest. She has to lie down to shoot it.

"To fire the weapon, you have to be prone," she says. "You have to lie down. That's why we have an A Gunner. You can't see anything, and the A Gunner gives me signals — right, left, up or down."

As she talks, a ladybug lands on her helmet.

"It's good luck," she says. "I'm a lucky lady."

And if she's lucky, she admits, she won't have to kill anybody.

Cpl. Miriam Jenkins

March 23, 2003

March 23, 2003

NAME: Michael McCarthy
RANK: Marine major
AGE: 39
HOMETOWN: Morton, Ill.
DUTY: Company commander, Charlie Company,
6th Engineer Support Battalion

Marine reservists focus on eve of combat

NORTHERN KUWAIT — Maj. Michael McCarthy stands before Charlie Company, looking at 125 Marines under his command.

"Good evening, Marines," he says.

The Marines circle around him, wearing protective pants and coats in case Iraq launches a preemptive biological or chemical attack. It is Wednesday, March 19, and tonight is the night it could happen.

The sun has gone down, and the camp is dark. Nobody is allowed to use white lights.

"How we doing?" he asks.

"Er!" the Marines yell together.

"Yeah, this is pretty freaky, isn't it?" he asks. "Glad to be out here with you. Glad to be out in front of Charlie Company."

McCarthy is a tall man, 6-foot-4, and built like a box, with rusty brown hair.

"For the folks who have been out here a while, great job; great job getting it ready for the battalion," McCarthy says.

A month ago, this forward staging area about 6 miles from the Iraqi border was nothing but sand.

Now, it's holding hundreds of Marines and equipment. Charlie Company helped build protective berms and bunkers in case of a Scud missile attack.

"Now, what I'm going to talk to you tonight about, in this lovely suit, is the fact that we are going to war," he says.

"Er!" the Marines yell together.

Almost all the Marines are reserves. They are teachers and firefighters and businessmen — everyday people who left their families back home. Few have seen combat.

For weeks, they've sat and waited, wondering when it was going to happen.

"Tonight, in about 20 minutes, 1st Marine Division is going to secure the oil fields," McCarthy says, looking at his watch.

His voice is calm, straightforward. He wants to set a tone, instill a sense of purpose, cut out the "B.S.," as he says. But he doesn't want the troops to peak too early.

"Thursday is D-Day plus 1," he says. "Fifth Corps will move forward."

He continues.

"Friday, at 1800, the air war will start. They'll put on a show for you."

He pauses again, moving slowly around the circle.

"Saturday, at 600, that's D-Day plus 3," he says. "Saturday is our day."

Most of the Marines are kneeling, holding M16 rifles. Charlie Company's mission is to transport and store fuel and water for the 1st Marine Expeditionary Force. Everyone is hoping this will be a quick war, but the tanks and vehicles can only go so long without getting fuel. If 6th ESB doesn't do its job, getting across the border, the war will come to a halt.

"Keep focused," McCarthy says. "Keep your eyes and ears open. Noncommissioned officers, I need you to drive your Marines."

He walks around the circle.

For the last six weeks, most of these Marines have been stationed at Camp Solomon Islands. They stayed in large white tents with electricity and power. They took showers in little buildings that look like mobile homes. They ate breakfast and supper every day in the chow hall.

The accommodations were like a Hilton compared to what's ahead for them.

The night before McCarthy's talk, they left Camp Solomon Islands and came here, a camp near the Iraq-Kuwait border, in a convoy of more than 100 vehicles. They didn't arrive until after 2 a.m., and some didn't get to sleep until just a few hours before dawn. There is no electricity. No chow hall. And the bathrooms are crude outhouses, built by Charlie Company, with drums of waste that have to be burned every day.

March 23, 2003

NAME: Chris Lomelino
RANK: Marine staff sergeant
AGE: 30
HOMETOWN: Davenport, Iowa
DUTY: Company gunnery sergeant, Charlie Company,
6th Engineer Support Battalion

McCarthy, who works full time in the product-support division at the world headquarters of Caterpillar Inc. in Peoria, Ill., has never seen combat. During Operation Desert Storm in 1991, he was in Japan. But after years of preparation, he's ready.

"Let's go," he says. "Let's do it."

"I'm excited to be here," he says. "I know you'll do great."

McCarthy asks whether his company staff has anything to add.

Staff Sgt. Chris Lomelino walks into the circle. He is intense, coiled and emotional — and complements McCarthy perfectly, by design.

"Things change fast," Lomelino says, his voice rising like that of a football coach talking to a group of teenagers. "We need to start thinking about moving with a purpose."

He didn't like the way the company came over for formation. They looked tired and slow, probably because few of the Marines had any sleep in the last two days. Now he wants to give them, as he calls it, a little verbal motivation.

"All I know is when I say go, all I'm going to see is freakin' butts and freakin' feet," Lomelino says. "All right?"

Lomelino, a construction worker from Davenport, Iowa, has never seen combat, but he, too, thinks he's ready.

"That's all I have."

"Errr!"

CAMOUFLAGE NETTING

TOWER

USMC

GARBAGE

SHOWER BAG

MAJORS TENT

SAND

CAMP VIPER ENGINEERS HQ

Major McCarthy's tent (foreground) and the 6th ESB command post tent (background) at Camp Viper.

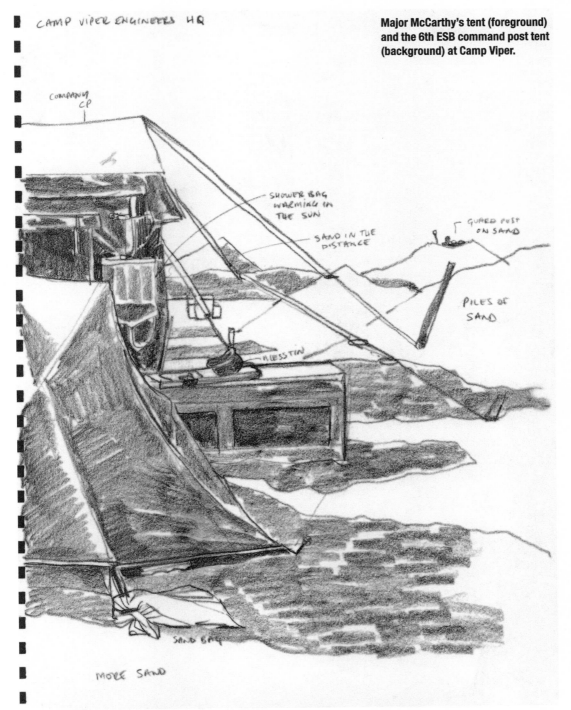

COMPANY CP

SHOWER BAG WARMING IN THE SUN

SAND IN THE DISTANCE

GUARD POST ON SAND

PILES OF SAND

KLESSTIN

SAND BAG

MORE SAND

April 5, 2003

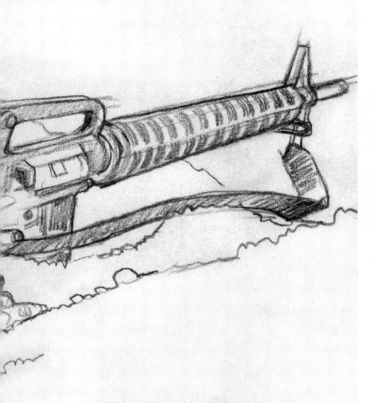

LANCE CORPORAL
DANIEL RHODES

March 27, 2003

CHAPTER 4

Raining Hell: 'Now, if something happens, are you scared to pull the trigger?'

March 23, 2003

NAME: T.R. Sparenberg
RANK: Marine sergeant
AGE: 26
HOMETOWN: Virginia, Ill.
DUTY: Squad leader of 14 Marines, Charlie Company,
6th Engineer Support Battalion

Sergeant provides refuge in midst of hell

CAMP CHESTY, central Iraq — Sgt. T.R. Sparenberg climbs into the truck with the presence of John Wayne and the rugged look of the Marlboro Man.

"Listen up," he says in a deep, serious voice. "If we see any civilians, you do not fire until I fire. I'll be the one who ends up in the psychiatrist's chair. If they are armed, go ahead and mess them up."

He pauses.

"Good to go?" he asks.

"Err!" the 14 Marines grunt back.

Good to go.

They ride in a 7-ton truck through the Iraqi desert, 14 Marines sitting shoulder to shoulder on a wooden box filled with explosives.

This is only one small squad of Marines, but it is about to deal with all of the major issues facing the entire U.S. military: Will Iraqi President Saddam Hussein use chemical weapons? Who will live or die? And how long will this war last in these awful conditions?

Sparenberg's squad is cruising across the desert with ease and bravado, heading north through enemy territory.

Led by this barrel-chested warrior, a Marine's Marine.

A rock of a man.

Sparenberg, 26, of Virginia, Ill., stands and studies the horizon, looking for Iraqis. He's so proud of his squad, to be riding into war with them. And he's promised each of their families that he'll bring them back.

Physically and emotionally.

"Being a 26-year-old Marine who has been in the Marine Corps for five years, I use the term 'psychiatrist's chair' when I talk about shooting a civilian," he says. "I'd rather have that on my shoulders than having an 18- or 19-year-old saying, 'Geez, what have I done?'

"I'm going to make that decision myself. If it's wrong, I'll pay the consequences."

SPARENBERG WALKS DOWN a row of white, two-person pup tents dug into the sand, waking up his squad: "Reveille!" he screams. "Reveille! Wake up, you baby killers!"

Everybody starts to laugh — nobody loves children more than Sparenberg, but he uses gallows humor to deal with the stress. Maybe it doesn't sound funny back home, where the war is reduced to sound bites and TV images that look like something out of a movie, but it does here, especially on a day like this, after you wake up and take a crap in a hole.

And your fingers are cracked and bleeding because the air is so dry.

And your hair is crusty from last night's sandstorm.

And you are about to spend another day in the same pair of underwear.

And your toenails are starting to rot.

And you feel like an animal, digging through the trash, scrounging for an empty water bottle to fill up.

And you're tired from being up all night on fire watch.

And you want a beer so bad you'd drink it warm.

And you sweat so much you don't bother with deodorant.

And you don't even know what day it is. Or what month.

And you don't know whether you are going to be alive tonight. And you are OK with that.

And the only thing that makes you happy is getting some mail.

And if you have another bag of Skittles, you are going to freak out because they come in almost every MRE (meals ready to eat).

And you're hungry because it's so damn hard to eat jambalaya for breakfast.

And you might have to kill somebody today.

And the most popular reading material is Maxim, Playboy or the really nasty stuff.

And you are carrying enough bullets to kill a small neighborhood.

And you don't even jump anymore when you hear an explosion.

And you have no idea when you are going home.

And you might have to kill somebody today.

Or maybe, you might give a little child some water, to try to start the healing process. But can one Marine really do anything to start something like that?

And your heart races when you hear a car horn, one of the signals of a gas attack, because you can't stand the thought of putting on your rubber boots and rubber gloves and gas mask again, considering it's 108 degrees — in the shade.

And everything you thought you knew, all the social norms, are gone, and the world has turned inside out.

And you might have to kill somebody today.

And you don't know whether your equipment is going to work because this is the Marines, and the Army gets all the money.

And you're so tired, so drained, so raw that you can have a complete conversation using only swear words with a few grunts thrown in for effect.

And you've grown so close to the guys in your squad, they feel like brothers. No, they are brothers. Maybe even closer.

AS THE MARINES get out of their tents and start to dig breakfast out of a box, they gather around Sparenberg. He sits on a camp stool, rising slightly above the others. He's a complicated man: cutting but painstakingly polite, strong and bold, decisive and certain. He attacks every issue straight on, with a healthy dose of sarcasm.

He puts his canteen cup on a fire, an old ammunition box converted into a camp stove with diesel fuel, warming some coffee.

Somehow, he makes all this chaos and absurdity feel normal. He's so strong, such a good guy. He's something to cling to when you are about to lose it.

IF EVERY WAR has music associated with it — Jimi Hendrix in Vietnam, for example — the theme song for Sparenberg's squad is "Gin and Juice."

They played it on a portable CD player while they waited to invade Iraq, listening on speakers held together with tape.

They played it at a camp in the middle of the desert while they got haircuts.

They played it while driving through the desert on a security patrol.

"Rollin' down the street, smokin indo, sippin' on gin and juice," Sparenberg sings. "Laid back! With my mind on my money and my money on my mind. Now, that, I got me some Seagram's gin. Everybody got the cups, but they ain't chipped in."

Sparenberg starts to dance like a cowboy. Like he just got off a bull. Legs bowed. Arms stiff but moving slightly above his shoulders. It's an old habit.

"Sippin' on gin and juice," he sings.

Before he joined the Marines, Sparenberg was a professional bull rider.

"I started riding bulls my senior year in high school," he says. "I needed an aggressive sport.

"I really enjoyed it and kind of excelled at it. Made

some money at it."

He traveled the rodeo circuit, competing mostly in the Midwest, but he quit last year.

"I thought I was getting too old to stay up with 18-year-olds," he says. "I get here, and I'm hanging out with 18-year-olds and doing the same thing they are. And I think I'm cheatin' myself."

Sparenberg tried college, but he developed a nasty drinking habit.

He was headed downhill, he says. "I needed something to do."

He went and saw a recruiter.

The recruiter happened to be a Marine, and Sparenberg signed up for six years. Just like that.

"It was the first office I walked into," Sparenberg says. "A lot of these Marines say they grew up wanting to become a Marine, and they feel their destiny was to be a Marine. Basically, I found mine as an accident. I don't regret it by any means. It was a great choice, and I stand behind it, and I love every minute of it."

Sparenberg was a child of divorce, so he was in no rush to get married.

"My mother and father divorced when I was 11 years old," he says. "My mother remarried and divorced again. Now, she's married to another guy who treats her quite well. My mother kept asking me why I didn't get married, and it's because I didn't want to get divorced."

Sparenberg and his wife, Amy, were married one day before he was deployed in January. They had been dating for 5½ years.

"It took an act of war to get me married," he says, jokingly.

Then, his voice drops to that dead-serious tone.

"It was the right thing to do. If anything hap-pened to me, I would want her to be taken care of. It also eased her mind. She can now call the unit and find out things that they won't tell a girlfriend.

"She can also receive other benefits. But that's not the reason I did it. It was the right thing to do. We lived together for about three years. Basically, we've been married that whole time."

He has wrapped tape around his wedding band, so it doesn't fall off.

"It fit my finger fine when we left," he says, "but I've lost some weight."

They are planning to have a big wedding ceremony when he returns.

"A military wedding," he says. Sparenberg plans to finish college, become a commissioned officer in the Marines and fly helicopters.

"Of course, I believe coming from the enlisted side, I would have an upper hand in leading Marines," he says. "I've been there and done that, as opposed to somebody who has done four years of college and walked right into it. In my opinion, that person could be clueless."

He has watched documentaries, learning about the great leaders in history, trying to copy some of their techniques.

"If my Marines don't have faith in themselves," he says, "I have faith in them."

AS HIS SQUAD PACKS the truck before leaving for Baghdad, a familiar song plays on the CD player.

Sparenberg and the 14 Marines in his squad sing along. It should be a scary moment, heading into Baghdad, but everybody is laughing and smiling, just like their leader.

"Sippin' on gin and juice," he sings.

LODA, ILL.
CORPORAL
CORY ROGERS
23

March 31, 2003

NAME: Corey Rogers
RANK: Marine corporal
AGE: 23
HOMETOWN: Loda, Ill.
DUTY: Combat engineer, Charlie Company,
6th Engineer Support Battalion

Sense of duty is corporal's main sustenance

CAMP CHESTY, central Iraq — Cpl. Corey Rogers keeps track of the missions on his T-shirt.

On his shoulder, it reads "Convoy Club: 13."

And counting.

After every convoy, he adds another mark with a pen.

"We pretty much got told we will be security on all the convoys — all of them, anywhere," he says.

In a two-week period, he has driven 790 miles through Iraq. Some are quick, three-hour trips. Others are eight, nine, 10 hours, as he stands watch behind a massive machine gun.

"There is a lot of desert," he says, smiling. "I had a different image of what we would be doing. They told us we would be up at Water Point doing security. I didn't know we'd be traveling like this."

Rogers operates a 240 Gulf, an accurate, powerful gun.

"It's kind of joked about, but you can use it as a sniper rifle because it's accurate at a mile," he says. "I've never shot anything that far."

After a few weeks in the desert, he had yet to fire his gun, so he went to a firing range. He found out that the weapon is not as accurate as he thought, shooting from the top of the Humvee.

"We have it jerry-rigged, on a tripod mounted on the top of the Humvee," he says. "We have to put up a better platform, because when you lean into it, you can move it all around the target. It's just sitting on the canvas. It's not sturdy."

Rogers joined the Marines on the advice of his grandfather, J.R. Herriott.

"My grandpa always told me that he thought it was everybody's duty to serve their country," Rogers says. "Everybody in my family has been in the Air Force — both my grandfathers, my dad, my brother, my great-grandpa. They didn't pressure me into it. He just told me that everybody should serve their country. My grandpas told me some stories, but they never told me the day-to-day routine."

So why did he join the Marines?

"I wanted to do it right," he says. "The Marines have given me some pretty good leadership and discipline. I've been in some pretty crappy situations here. You eat crappy food, and it's hard work and you are expected to do the job. It's like construction. When I was roofing, I did the same thing."

Rogers is a combat engineer with Charlie Company, 6th Engineer Support Battalion.

"When I first started, I looked at this squad," he says. "I thought, this kind of sucks. I didn't know them very well. Most of the guys I hung around with are in different squads. But now, I think we have the best squad. We always work together, and we have diversity. A lot of the other squads are bickering."

He joined in May 1999.

"I just like to build stuff and go out shooting sometimes," he says. "And I like to blow stuff up. It's a new experience. Parts have sucked, like when we were on guard for a week straight, eight on and eight off. It wasn't bad because we got on a routine, but it sucked sitting there for eight hours at a time."

Roberts, who is a reservist, graduated recently from Illinois State University with a degree in construction management.

"I like construction," Rogers says. "I figured if I don't like construction, I can always be a cop. And if I don't like being a cop, I can always go back to construction."

He's pretty certain he will be able to land a job, being a veteran and having a college degree. "I should be near the top," he says.

PFC.
ALEX LEWIS BUHLMAN

March 28, 2003

NAME: Alex Buhlman
RANK: Marine private 1st class
AGE: 19
HOMETOWN: Farmington Hills, Mich.
DUTY: Combat engineer, Charlie Company,
6th Engineer Support Battalion

Adventure lured Marine to join force

SOUTHERN IRAQ — Pfc. Alex Buhlman was watching the History Channel when he saw a show on combat engineers.

"It showed what the combat engineers did in World War II," says Buhlman, 19, of Farmington Hills, Mich. "The engineers stopped an advancement by blowing up a bridge. I thought, 'Man, that looks cool.' "

It stuck in his head.

When he joined the Marine Reserve, he wanted to become a combat engineer.

"We do a lot of cool stuff, like build things and blow things up," he says.

Buhlman, fresh out of boot camp, is sitting on a sand berm in southern Iraq, protecting a supply base.

"A lot of guys say, 'He's fresh, just out of boot camp, what does he know?' " Buhlman says. "But I just had all the training and I haven't had time to forget it. It took me awhile to gain their trust. I think they got used to me, and I got used to them."

Buhlman is with Charlie Company, 6th Engineer Support Battalion.

"When I was little, I remember watching the first war, being really interested in it," Buhlman says. "For some reason, I remember eating Pizza Hut pizza, watching the gulf war."

It's strange, the things you remember 12 years later, when you are half a world away from childhood.

"There's a big difference," he says. "When you see it on television, you think it's tanks and planes, and the ground troops don't do much. You think it's all mechanized. But you don't think about bunker clearing."

Buhlman has done his share of bunker clearing, approaching a sand bunker with a shotgun to find out whether it's occupied by the enemy.

"It's a scary moment, but to this point, none of the bunkers has been filled," Buhlman says.

"When we crossed the border into Iraq, I was thinking, 'I hope we'll be all right. I hope we don't see anything.' But it was really exciting. Everybody was alert and awake, locked and loaded.

"I'm all about experiences. Life's about experiences. I'm not a real church guy, but I think life is more about learning than staying away from sin."

Buhlman was born in Shreveport, La., where he lived for a year. He grew up in Farmington Hills. His family moved to Bel Air, Md., where he went to high school. In June, the family moved back to Farmington Hills.

He signed up for the Marine Reserve midway through his senior year of high school.

"I wanted the experience. I wanted something exciting; I joined at the right time, I guess."

Buhlman has gone nonstop since graduating from high school.

"It's been a big rush," he says.

He drove to Maryland for boot camp on June 24. He graduated on Sept. 20 and then had a 10-day leave, so he went back to Michigan. After four weeks of combat training, he had seven weeks of combat-engineer school. He got out Dec. 14 and drove back to Michigan for a week.

He drove back to Maryland for his first drill weekend, where he learned that he had been activated.

"I didn't get a chance to say good-bye to my family," he says.

So his family went to see him.

"My parents were pretty calm," he says. "My dad would let out a sigh, like, 'Oh, man.' He couldn't believe his son was going to war. I'm sure there were tears, but there was nothing frantic."

When he gets back, he plans to buy his dream car, a red 1970s Corvette Stingray with a T-top.

"I've been looking for about a year," he says. "That's the first thing that I'm going to get. I've been thinking about it since boot camp, and that seems like a lifetime ago."

LANCE CORPORAL SIDNEY MENDOZA

April 4, 2003

NAME: Sidney Mendoza
RANK: Marine lance corporal
AGE: 26
HOMETOWN: San Jose, Calif.
DUTY: Combat engineer, Charlie Company,
6th Engineer Support Battalion

Marine defends adopted land

CAMP VIPER, southern Iraq — Lance. Cpl. Sidney Mendoza was in a truck heading through the Iraqi desert when he heard a loud bang.

"I guess we went over a land mine," Mendoza says. "I remember thinking somebody shot at me. That was the wildest moment because I didn't know what it was. I was ready to shoot back, at whoever it was."

Mendoza is the gunner for a .50-caliber machine-gun team. It's his job to load the gun, spot where the rounds go and adjust fire.

"All I remember was, I was wanting to get up there, load the babies in on the .50 cal and shoot at whoever was shooting, so they wouldn't be shooting at us any more," Mendoza says.

Mendoza, a combat engineer assigned to Charlie Company, 6th Engineer Support Battalion, joined the Marine Reserve after Sept. 11, 2001.

"At that point in time, I started to think, 'You know what, America has given me so much,'" he says. "And I decided to join the Marines."

Mendoza was born in Nicaragua, and his family moved to San Jose, Calif., when he was 3.

"My parents have been able to live the American dream," he says. "I'm really grateful for America and all the opportunity that's been given to me."

He became a U.S. citizen when he was 19.

"That was the proudest day of my life," he says.

Mendoza lived in San Jose for 20 years. He went to Silver Creek High School and then graduated from San Jose State University with a degree in mar-keting. He decided to become a minister and spent a year in the seminary.

"I ended up dropping out because it got expensive," he says.

After leaving the seminary, he bounced from job to job, unable to find the right fit. He tried sales but didn't like it.

"Right before I got activated, I was working with a friend of my dad in Arizona," he says. "He does income taxes for the Hispanic community, and he opens up franchises. I was going through the process of having my own location to do income taxes, to learn the ropes. Then, I was going to open income tax businesses, and then I would get a cut from each business. But that plan went out the door for now."

Mendoza married his longtime girlfriend, Martha Garcia, one week before he was deployed. Her father, the Rev. Hugo Garcia, performed the ceremony in a chapel in Oceanside, Calif., not far from Camp Pendleton.

"It wasn't as cool as I'd like," he says. "I didn't have any friends or family there."

The conditions in the desert are rough, but he tries to keep a positive attitude.

"I try to look at the bright side," he says. "I have food every day. I have shelter. I'm alive. I'm just doing my job. You can't be out here and think, 'I hate this every day.' It wears on you.

"If I die, I know I'm going to heaven. But nobody wants to die. I want to go back home and start a family."

March 31, 2003

NAME: Timothy Edwards
RANK: Marine lance corporal
AGE: 24
HOMETOWN: Fremont, Wis.
DUTY: Truck driver, Charlie Company,
6th Engineer Support Battalion

Religion is Marine's driving force

CAMP VIPER, southern Iraq — Lance Cpl. Timothy Edwards wrote his nickname on his helmet: Preacher.

Edwards, 24, of Fremont, Wis., is a youth minister and plans to become a pastor.

"I get a lot of mail from the kids I work with," Edwards says. "That's the stuff that cheers me up the most. The kids remember me and tell me how good I was. It makes me feel good about what I was doing."

A reservist, Edwards is a truck driver assigned to Charlie Company, 6th Engineer Support Battalion. He drives many types of trucks, including dump trucks.

"These new trucks are kind of like driving a car," Edwards says. "It's all push-button. It's pretty nice. The old trucks are a little more tricky. Stuff breaks, and you have to be semi-mechanically oriented. You can fix it."

Edwards tries to maintain his Christian ways in a place where profanity is as common as sand.

"I can't judge other people for swearing," Edwards says. "Sometimes, it's just the way they vent their frustrations."

March 15, 2003

NAME: Steffen Melvin
RANK: Marine corporal
AGE: 32
HOMETOWN: Hartford, Mich.
DUTY: Bulk-fuel specialist, 6th Engineer Support Battalion

Marine relies on lessons of first gulf war

NORTHERN KUWAIT — Cpl. Steffen Melvin sits outside a two-person tent, eating Skittles. He tries to relax and conserve his energy, after hearing radio reports that the bombing in Iraq has started. And he knows, soon, he will cross the border.

"Thank God, we are finally getting something started," he says, popping a candy into his mouth. Most Marines are sick of the Skittles that seem to come in every prepackaged MRE, or meals ready to eat. But Melvin needs the sugar for what's ahead.

"We can hurry up, get it done and get home," he says. Melvin, 32, a Marine from Hartford, Mich., is a bulk-fuel specialist with the 6th Engineer Support Battalion.

For now, the Marines can do nothing but wait until they are sent across the Iraqi border. They clean their weapons, pack and pack again.

Melvin hasn't showered for 10 days — he thinks. Truth is, he can't remember. After a certain point, it hardly matters. Everything he owns is stuffed inside two bags, lying in the dirt. He is covered in sand and dust.

"All that matters is: We are going that way," he says, pointing north toward the Iraq border, about 6 miles away. "When we punch across the border, there is a possibility that we will encounter Iraqis. I don't know if they'll be hostile or not."

Melvin was in the 1991 Persian Gulf War. His unit saw minor skirmishes but not a lot of heavy combat.

"We walked through the burning oil fields for a day," he remembers. "Your feet were raw, red and bleeding the entire time. Your back hurt like hell the entire time.

"It was no big deal at the time. It was what we did. Nobody really thought about it at the time. It was hot, and it was long."

When the first gulf war started, Melvin, who is 5 feet 6, weighed 155 pounds. But food was scarce, and he wasted away, losing 25 pounds.

Melvin grew up an Army brat. His father, Douglas Melvin, died of polio at 32. "He was a big guy," Melvin says. "Never complained."

Steffen Melvin joined the Marines when he was 17. "I turned 19 over here the first time," he says. "And I turned 32 over here this time." He is in charge of four Marines, and he's tried to prepare them for taking prisoners of war.

"In the first gulf war, when we came across the border, we started taking POWs," he says. "It was eerie. You come over a hill, and there is a bunch of them. They outnumber you, and as soon as you see them, they drop everything they have and put their hands in the air. They didn't want to play. They were forced to be there. They knew they were out-trained, outgunned."

He is one of the few Marines at this forward staging area who have experience. "I tell my guys to pay attention to detail," he says. "It will keep you alive when rounds start coming your direction."

Melvin, who builds and maintains electrical power lines in Phoenix, Ariz., joined the reserves in September 2002.

"I wanted to be involved," he says. "I'm still young enough and capable enough to perform. I have a little experience, and maybe I can keep some of these young kids out of trouble."

Melvin hopes his own children, Christian, 10, and Nicholas, 6, learn from his actions.

"I wanted to show them there are things more important in life than yourself," he says. "If there are things, if you believe in them strong enough, no matter the consequences, you have to do them."

As the day approaches when this battalion will head to war, Melvin has a certain calm.

"I'm 12 years older," he says. "The first time, I was cockier, more arrogant. ... Still confident to a fault sometimes. And I'm more cautious. I worry more about my guys than myself sometimes."

March 27, 2003

NAME: Daniel Rhodes
RANK: Marine lance corporal
AGE: 22
HOMETOWN: Champaign, Ill.
DUTY: Combat engineer, Charlie Company,
6th Engineer Support Battalion

Reservist has all he'll ever need

CAMP VIPER, southern Iraq — For two hours, Lance Cpl. Daniel Rhodes lies on the ground holding an M16 rifle. His left elbow is aching. Half his body is numb. Both knees hurt. Two grenades stick in his ribs. A canteen rubs against his hip.

His Kevlar helmet rides low on his forehead, and he has to push it back to see. He's on a team, spread across the desert, providing security for combat engineers, who are about to blow up part of a road in southern Iraq.

Rhodes spots some Iraqi civilians in the distance, about 1,000 meters away, walking toward his position.

"What are they doing?" Rhodes wonders.

He grips the M16 tightly. The rifle can hold 30 rounds, one in the chamber and 29 in the magazine. But he's using only 25 today, so the spring doesn't jam with sand.

He counts three civilians.

He sees a man on a donkey, waving his arms wildly, like he's throwing a grenade.

The man wears traditional Iraqi clothing with a scarf draped around his neck.

The other two people are smaller. They look like a child and a woman wearing hoods or scarves over their heads.

Rhodes has been warned about Iraqi commandos wearing civilian clothing. They lull you into a false sense of security and then take you prisoner.

Or worse.

He assumes the worst. Maybe the man has forced the woman and child to walk with him, to provide cover.

Or maybe they are trying to surrender.

"The United States dropped leaflets, telling the Iraqis how to surrender, but maybe the message didn't translate," Rhodes thinks.

Rhodes has been preparing for this moment since he was in high school. He has always wanted to be a Marine, and has always expected to end up in the Middle East. He took Arabic in college, but he can't really speak it.

The family keeps getting closer.

"Maybe this is what they always do," Rhodes thinks. "Maybe this is their backyard and they are looking for their sheep. Maybe this isn't so strange; maybe this is part of their culture, walking back and forth. In America, we go boom! straightforward."

But he doesn't know. And that's the dilemma.

"We are trying to free these people, but we are in a catch-22," Rhodes thinks. "You are trying to grant these people freedom from an oppressive government; at the same time, you have to be careful, because you don't know who is working for that government."

RHODES HAS ALWAYS been infatuated with the Marines. When he was in kindergarten, he had two sets of camouflage clothing. He would refuse to put on anything else. He'd wear one set, and then change into the other while the first pair was being washed.

Rhodes, a former high school All-American gymnast, lies perfectly still. He is strong, dedicated, and he's come to grips with the fact that he might have to shoot a civilian.

A man. Or a woman. Or a child, armed with a gun.

"If I don't, somebody could die."

Rhodes was brought up in an extremely religious household. When he left for college, his parents, Connie and David Rhodes, sold their house and cars and headed for South America. They are missionaries who run an orphanage in Lima, Peru. They were giving him money for college until he found out it was money they should have been using to eat.

He tried to work full time as a truck driver while going to school. "I was killing myself," he says. "So I joined the Marine Reserve. It all fell into place. I needed discipline. The Marines really kicked me in the butt, and I needed it."

Rhodes is a student at the University of Illinois at Urbana-Champaign, studying political science. He stays with six other guys — all of them want to become Marines — in a house called the Pit. "It's not a fraternity," he says. "It's a tight group of guys with the same intentions. It's rowdy as heck. The house is utter chaos."

The perfect training ground for a Marine. Every room is decorated with Marine recruiting posters. A belt of 762mm machine gun rounds hangs from the chandelier.

Rhodes had planned to go to officer candidate school this summer, but the war put those plans on hold. When he graduates from college, he will be commissioned a second lieutenant and go on active duty in the Marines. He plans to put in 20 years and then go into politics. He'd like to be a senator someday.

THE SAFETY IS OFF, but his finger is not on the trigger — not until he's ready to fire.

The man whips the donkey to move faster.

Sgt. T.R. Sparenberg tries to wave the man off. "Get out of here," he screams.

The danger is increasing, but Rhodes isn't afraid. "I've pretty much accepted the fact that I won't come home or I probably won't be coming home with all my parts. If I come home with everything, it's a bonus."

But the man continues to approach. "If you come too close, we don't know what to do," Rhodes says. "Even though we are spread out, if he comes within 20 meters, he could take a lot of us out with a grenade."

Rhodes has never felt so alive. He wakes up excited about being here. "This is what I'm good at," he says. "I'm full of energy. At home, I'm exhausted. Going to class and doing bills, that's not for me. I'm more scared of civilian life than being here.

"The Marines is everything I need. This is what I thought it would be, a bunch of rough-cut guys who say what they think, all with cockiness and attitude. I just like the attitude."

Not everything has gone perfectly. Rhodes is afraid that his parents haven't accepted that he's in Iraq. When he left, his family said things like, "Hopefully, you'll be building bathrooms in the rear or in the United States."

He told them repeatedly, "If it happens, I'll be in Iraq."

He had been in Kuwait for 25 days when he received a letter from them, asking how he was doing in California. He wrote a letter to his sister, telling her to talk to his parents, to convince them that he's in Iraq.

The man is just 30 meters away when he stops. He turns around and leaves.

"Why did he just do that?" Rhodes says, getting angry. "You start to think, I could have taken him out if I would have misinterpreted something he did."

The scene repeats itself over and over, all across the desert, as the Marines try to pick out the commandos from the civilians.

"Man, I could have shot him," Rhodes says. "And that defeats the purpose of why we are here."

LANCE CORPORAL
DANIEL RHODES

March 27, 2003

March 23, 2003

NAME: Bob Martin
RANK: Marine corporal
AGE: 22
HOMETOWN: Peoria, Ill.
DUTY: Combat engineer, Charlie Company,
6th Engineer Support Battalion

Machine-gunner setting sights on danger

CAMP VIPER, southern Iraq — Cpl. Bob Martin stands in a U-shaped machine-gun nest, dug in the sand, staring at a crest in the desert.

He's heard there is a battalion of Iraqi soldiers lurking nearby in armored vehicles, somewhere to the south.

"If they are coming, they are coming right over that crest," he says to two Marines on watch with him.

He squints into a pair of binoculars. Nothing there.

A strong wind kicks up a blinding sandstorm. He puts on a pair of goggles caked with dust and dirt. He leans into a machine gun that launches grenades.

He gets out an AT4, an antitank rocket, and lays it on the sand. He jokes that it's "Marine proof" — with pictures on the side on how to hold it, how to aim and how to fire.

But there is one rule when trying to bring down a tank: The closer you are, the better.

So he sits and waits.

Martin, 22, of Peoria, Ill., is a combat engineer. He is guarding a crucial supply camp, which will provide fuel to about 50,000 Marines. The war rages around him. He's heard reports about some troops who were captured and others who died, but he hasn't seen a battle up close yet.

"Every day here is worse than the day before," he says. "I'm sick of waiting for something to happen. We are just waiting for somebody to come over that crest. We want to be part of the war."

He scoops up a chunk of sand and crushes it in his fingertips.

"I just got a letter from my mom," Martin says to a Marine. "They caught bin Laden's right-hand man, the guy who planned the World Trade Center attacks."

The news is weeks old, but it seems brand new. In the age of the Internet, these young Marines have never been so out of touch.

And Martin has never been so tired. That's the one thing he misses, a full night of sleep. Last night, he got about four hours after a sergeant woke him up and told him to help strip a 7-ton truck in the dark, removing the roof and benches, turning it into a flatbed truck.

He has no idea why.

"It would be a lot easier if they told us what our mission was," he says.

For weeks, he has worked security — eight hours on, eight hours off, eight hours on again.

Martin sleeps on the ground, in a sleeping bag, inside a waterproof shell. The Marines in Charlie Company move so much they don't bother to put up tents. And the truth is, he doesn't mind it.

Every morning after breakfast, he takes the blue pill, as the Marines call it, a medicine to prevent malaria.

Standing 5 feet 10 and weighing 180 pounds, he figures he has lost about 15 pounds eating MREs, or meals ready to eat.

Back home in Peoria, Ill., Martin, who is a Marine reservist, is a surveillance officer at a department store. When he gets out of Iraq, he plans to finish his studies at Illinois State University. He's studying business administration and wants to run his own business.

Martin is convinced he will be home in July because reservists get additional benefits if they are gone for more than 180 days. Charlie Company was activated Jan. 15. Earlier that January day, he married Brooke Martin.

"We went down to the courthouse and got married. We are still gonna have the big wedding when I get back."

In his combat vest, he keeps a pair of her pink panties in a plastic bag. She sprayed them with his favorite perfume.

March 23, 2003

"It smells sort of like grapes," he says.

When everybody else in his squad saw the bag and smelled the perfume, they wrote home, asking their wives and girlfriends to send the same thing.

"It's been so long since I smelled a woman," he says.

Two Chinook helicopters fly by, carrying troops and equipment, right over the crest he's been watching.

"If there was a battalion out there, sure as heck, these Chinooks wouldn't be out there," he says.

His shoulders relax. He leans against his gun and takes another breath of sand.

April 4, 2003

NAME: Paul Sailer
RANK: Marine lance corporal
AGE: 22
HOMETOWN: Pekin, Ill.
DUTY: Combat engineer, Charlie Company,
6th Engineer Support Battalion

Marine is on edge in his desert digs

CAMP VIPER, southern Iraq — Lance Cpl. Paul Sailer is on watch, late at night, trying to stay alert. He won't fall asleep, no way, not after what happened years ago.

"I fell asleep on watch a long time ago and learned my lesson," Sailer says. "They made me dig a grave for myself, 6 foot by 6 foot. Took me all day. I was sweating big time when I was done, and it taught me a lesson."

Sailer, 22, of Pekin, Ill., is a combat engineer with Charlie Company, 6th Engineer Support Battalion.

"This ain't so bad," he says. "There's not much to it. I get up, stand guard duty or fill sandbags and go to bed."

He is stationed in southern Iraq, facing miserable conditions from 100-degree heat to sandstorms.

The Marines use a crude outhouse, under a camouflage net. It's a two-seat wooden platform, over a hole in the sand.

Two Marines can sit back to back. But that's not the strange part. The thing you don't forget is how the flies come up from the hole. "The flies don't bother me," he says. "The ladybugs give me more of a problem. They fly into my face."

The Marines sleep in two-person pup tents or under the stars in a bivey bag, a Gortex cocoon around a sleeping bag.

"That's pretty comfortable as long as you dig up the sand under the tent before you go to bed," he says.

They eat MREs, or meals ready to eat, prepackaged meals that include everything from a main course to fruit. The Marines joke that every MRE comes with a package of peanut butter and Skittles.

"I've hated MREs since boot camp," Sailer says. "They are horrible. They all taste exactly the same, either bland or Tabasco sauce. There's no difference."

For the last 2½ weeks, the Marines have worn the same biochem suits every day. Almost everybody has ripped or torn their suit, and the holes are covered with duct tape.

"My suit doesn't fit me," Sailer says. "I just kind of try to strap it real tight."

What sets Sailer apart is the big, brown hat he wears constantly.

"I wear the hat because my head would fry," he says. "My hands and arms aren't so bad, but my neck would fry."

After countless Scud drills and gas-attack warnings — everybody has to put on their full biochem gear including a gas mask, rubber gloves and rubber boots, which is exhausting in the heat. Everybody is on edge. If a car horn goes off or if somebody screams, everybody jumps or reaches for their gas mask.

"Not much bothers me out here," he says. "But most of it is the hurry up and wait. They say, 'We are going to leave in 5 minutes.' We are going to leave in 5 minutes, and then 10 hours later, you still aren't gone. Everything gets fumbled. Everything gets packed in the wrong place. When they want you to find something in a hurry, it's like, 'Man, where did I put that?'"

Sailer joined the Marine Corps Reserve in 1999.

"I was bored," he says. "I was just about to graduate from high school, and I had nothing to do. A recruiter called and I said, 'Sure, I'll come down.'"

Less than a month later, he was in the delayed entry program.

"At the time, it was my parents' influence," he says. "If I had to do it over, I would have gone active, not reserves. My dad was all for it, but my mom wanted me to stay home and go to college."

He studies pre-law at Illinois Central College. He plans to transfer to Illinois State University when he returns home.

"I miss music and alcohol," he says. "I miss vodka. That's the way to go. And I miss hanging out with my friends, just normal life, so I don't have to worry about anybody shooting my butt."

Cpl. Brian Hooley

April 2, 2003

NAME: Brian Hooley
RANK: Marine corporal
AGE: 23
HOMETOWN: Hannibal, Mo.
DUTY: Driver/heavy- equipment operator,
6th Engineer Support Battalion

NAME: Troy Turnbull
RANK: Marine corporal
AGE: 28
HOMETOWN: Springfield, Ill.
DUTY: Driver/welder,
6th Engineer Support Battalion

Truck drivers head north into danger

SOUTHERN IRAQ — Before heading into the heart of Iraq, Cpl. Brian Hooley turns to Cpl. Troy Turnbull.

"Now, if something happens, are you scared to pull the trigger?" Hooley asks.

"I don't think so," Turnbull says. "I think I can handle it."

But he doesn't know. These two truck drivers have never seen combat, and now they are in a convoy heading north in Iraq.

Hooley is driving a 5-ton truck filled with explosives and demolition charges. Turnbull is in the passenger seat. Two Marines are in the back of the truck, manning a .50-caliber machine gun mounted on top.

Before leaving, Hooley and Turnbull were warned that the road is unsecured. There is word of enemy positions along the route, and anything could happen.

"They told us if any civilian vehicles come into the convoy, run them off the road," says Hooley, who's in the Marine Corps Reserve. In his regular job, he works as a crane operator in Hannibal, Mo. He is married and has three children.

"They've had problems with civilian vehicles trying to bust up convoys. And if anybody so much as lifts a weapon toward us, we are supposed to light them up."

The convoy comes to a stop, although Hooley doesn't know why. At the lower ranks, Marines never seem to know why anything happens.

Hooley gets out of the truck and talks to the two Marines in back. He makes sure they are all right and that the load hasn't shifted.

He stops and says jokingly, "I'm going to get back in the truck before somebody snipes me."

Hooley gets in the truck and notices several Marines looking at something behind the convoy.

"Look at this, these Marines are aimed in," Hooley says to Turnbull.

A white Toyota pickup is coming up a dirt road, approaching on the left flank, from the rear, but there is a herd of sheep in the middle of the road. The shepherds are trying to get them out of the way, whacking them with sticks. Two small children and a woman help herd the sheep.

Hooley turns to say something to Turnbull and hears a gunshot from the pickup.

Hooley grabs his M16 rifle. The pickup is nearly 219 yards away, well within range. He aims his first shot at the driver's-side windshield. He shoots again. A guy gets out of the pickup, and Hooley fires a third time. He's pretty sure he hit the hood of the truck.

His rifle jams twice, but he just fires again.

Another guy gets out of the Toyota. Hooley fires one shot at the man's head, but he doesn't know if it hit him, because there are so many tracer rounds flying through the air.

"I'd say there were well over 50 people shooting," he said later. "It was raining lead. It was unbelievable. It was about 25 seconds, but it felt like a half-hour when you are sitting there firing."

The guy falls to the ground, and Hooley fires another shot at the center of his body.

Turnbull grabs his gun, lurches across the seat and sticks it out the driver's-side window, leaning on Hooley's back.

"Do you mind if I get in here?" he asks. A reservist, Turnbull works in a warehouse in Springfield, Ill. He is married and has four children.

"Go ahead."

Turnbull squeezes off a shot, less than 6 inches from Hooley's ear.

"Cease fire!" somebody yells.

Turnbull is locked in for another shot, but he hears the call again: "Cease fire!"

Hooley jumps down and crosses the road to a more secure location. Then Turnbull gets down and takes a position next to his partner.

April 2, 2003

The Toyota is riddled with bullets. The windshield is shattered. Both headlights are blown to bits. Two tires are flat.

Two Iraqis are dead; one is wounded, and the Marines take five enemy prisoners of war (EPWs). No Marines are injured. The Iraqis got off only one shot.

A 15-year-old girl broke her neck and died diving into a ditch, according to a public affairs officer at 6th Engineer Support Battalion command.

A gun was never found, but the Marines believe the shooting came from the Toyota and the gun was dumped to one of the civilians.

Hooley sees six dead sheep and remembers the woman and children.

"Are the children all right?" Hooley asks.

"Yes," a staff sergeant says. "The mom and kids are OK."

A medevac, or medical evacuation unit, helicopter picks up the injured EPWs.

"If it's gonna be you or them, we are gonna go home to our families," Hooley says.

That night, Hooley and Turnbull complete the mission. Hooley feels like his senses are supercharged, like he could look out 300 yards and determine if somebody has a stick in his hand or a weapon.

The convoy reaches its destination, a supply camp in a dangerous setting farther north.

They try to sleep in the truck, but they are too wired. They are both eager for more action.

Hooley is asked whether he will tell this story over and over, someday, sitting in a bar.

"I don't know if I'll talk about stuff like this in a bar," he says. "Not many people know what it's like to be in an area where they have to kill or be killed, or even stand up for something they believe in."

Turnbull finishes his thought: "If they didn't have people like us to volunteer, the United States would be in bad shape, wouldn't it?"

GUNNERY SERGEANT
ROD RICHARDS
DUG UP MINE WITH AN
MRE SPOON

March 27, 2003

NAME: Rod Richards
RANK: Marine gunnery sergeant
AGE: 34
HOMETOWN: Morton, Ill.
DUTY: Platoon commander, Charlie Company,
6th Engineer Support Battalion

Unseen enemy has hearts racing

CAMP VIPER, southern Iraq — Approaching a massive Iraqi bunker system that can hold up to 1,000 soldiers, Gunnery Sgt. Rod Richards expects to face a nasty firefight.

Or maybe he will find hundreds of dead bodies, if the Air Force beat him to it.

A few weeks ago, he was told the bunker was occupied.

"When the unit was given its mission, it looked bleak," he says.

At best, Richards is hoping hundreds of Iraqis will surrender to a couple squads of Marines.

Richards, a platoon commander overseeing 46 Marines, is in charge of flank security for a convoy heading north through Iraq. Using satellite pictures, they mapped out the bunker system in a sandbox and developed a plan of attack.

Richards rides in a 7-ton truck with 15 Marines, loaded with several types of guns. He is also in charge of another 7-ton truck with another squad of Marines led by Sgt. Kenneth Ferguson. The two trucks will provide security for a team that will clear the bunker. As they approach the bunker, nobody is around. Everything is destroyed. There is no sign of life. No sign of death, either.

"It looks abandoned," Richards says.

They stop, and a few guys go to the bathroom. They've been driving for 10 hours.

Richards looks through binoculars at small bunkers, which could probably hold about four soldiers, built into the sand.

Richards directs his truck crew to approach the bunkers with guns ready to fire, but again, nobody is around.

The truck takes off and somebody screams: "Yee haw!"

A few minutes later, Ferguson spots a tank turret on the horizon, probably 875 yards away, north of the convoy they're protecting.

Richards sees the turrets through binoculars and calls command.

"There's a turret facing me, making me nervous," Ferguson says.

Richards' trucks are in the open, in the middle of the desert, well within range of a tank.

"I have two options," Richards thinks. "Being spotted driving away and being blown to bits, or being spotted while attacking and being blown to bits."

He decides to attack.

"If everything goes really well, we will lose a fire team or so," Richards thinks. Only four Marines would die.

If things go bad, he thinks, almost nobody would survive. His mission is to clear the area. If he fails, more than 80 people in the convoy could die.

Richards asks Ferguson for his attack recommendation.

Richards will take the tank on the left. Ferguson will focus on the tank on the right.

Two squads of engineers are about to attack two main battle tanks. They are carrying four antitank rockets, machine guns and C4 explosives rigged with 10-second fuses.

The trucks race across the desert toward the tanks, but the turrets don't move.

Richards' truck parks about 275 yards away from the tank.

Richards can see the turret, hidden behind a berm, protected with barbed wire. His squad fans out across the desert and sets up the machine guns.

"Things are going well," Richards thinks.

Ferguson calls in more intelligence: A third tank has been spotted.

Richards is working the radio. He tries to give the grid coordinates for air support, but the radio is cluttered with chatter. Someone from 1st Platoon is trying to tell Explosive Ordnance Disposal the location where they found some unexploded ordnance. A

Richards
writing letters
in Camp Viper.

March 27, 2003

support platoon driver asks another driver if he had eaten noon chow.

Richards is furious.

"I'd smash their face in, with a smile, if I could reach them," he thinks. It's an uncommon burst of anger. Richards is normally mild-mannered. A Marine reservist, he is a father of two who works in information technology.

Richards is losing $1,500 a month by not working his regular job.

"You can always make more money," he says. "Being away from the kids is the only real loss."

He's about to miss both of their birthdays. Abby will be 4 in three weeks, while Riley will be 1 in a month.

Richards is one of the few Marines in Charlie Company, 6th Engineer Support Battalion, with combat experience. He did four months of active duty in the first Persian Gulf War, as a squad leader.

He saw the first war as a grand adventure. With this one, he's only concerned about his Marines.

Four Marines run up to the tank with guns and explosives, knowing they will probably not survive. They will be mowed down by machine-gun fire or they won't find cover in time to get protection from the 10-second fuse on the block of explosive.

Right before setting off the explosives, they discover the tank is a clever decoy.

Richards is proud of his Marines.

"Not too bad for our first encounter with a tank," he says.

A FEW HOURS LATER, Richards rides on the same truck, providing flank security for the convoy. The truck is about 250 yards off the road, churning through soft sand. Richards notices a rusty brown metal disc half buried in the sand. The disc disappears under the truck. Richards looks up and sees hundreds of little discs spread across the ground.

Land mines!

"Stop!" Richards screams.

The truck comes to a stop, and Sgt. T.R. Sparenberg sighs.

Richards calls command: They have driven into a minefield.

Richards hops out, carefully. He digs around the disc with a plastic spoon, trying to find out whether it is connected to an explosive. He's pretty sure it's an antitank mine. "They go off from pressure," he thinks.

He should be good to go, working under the disc.

He doesn't feel anything under the disc and with one quick move, he flips it on its side.

Nothing happens.

It's a fake, and he smiles.

Another Marine finds another type of land mine, small ones called Toe Poppers, which blow off your foot.

Even if one land mine is a fake, they don't know about the others.

They drive the truck backward, out of the minefield. But there is a trailer on back, and it starts to jackknife.

"Stop!" somebody screams. "Turn the wheels the other way!"

Richards walks across the ground, leading the truck out of the minefield, and they reach safety.

"Fake mines, fake tanks," Richards says. "Someday, somebody isn't going to cry wolf."

March 23, 2003

NAME: Jeremy Janssen
RANK: Marine lance corporal
AGE: 20
HOMETOWN: Dwight, Ill.
DUTY: Combat engineer,
6th Engineer Support Battalion

Scud alerts make service surreal

BREACH POINT, northern Kuwait — "Incoming Scud!" somebody yells. "Gas! Gas! Gas!"

Lance Cpl. Jeremy Janssen puts on his gas mask and runs across the base, past pup tents and a portable water container, and reaches a bunker, about 4 feet wide, 4 feet underground. The roof is covered with sandbags.

It is March 20, a long, exhausting day for the Marines in the 6th Engineer Support Battalion. The sky is so thick with sand you can look at the sun without sunglasses. The temperature is unbearable.

"Everybody in the bunkers!" somebody screams.

Janssen sits in the bunker on the cold sand, wearing rubber boots, rubber gloves, a gas mask and a biochemical suit. All he hears is the hiss-pop of 10 Marines and two journalists breathing in gas masks.

The U.S. Army shoots off a Missile Launching Rocket System. Janssen gets up and looks out of the bunker. Missiles shoot into the air, and there is a loud explosion.

"You guys hear that?" Janssen screams.

Janssen cracks some jokes. When people get scared, he tries to calm them down.

"Incoming Scud!" somebody screams over the radio. "Scud. Scud. Scud."

Another missile streaks through the sky, leaving a trail of smoke. The Marines assume it's a cruise missile.

Janssen stands outside the bunker, watching the light show. Yeah, that was impressive, Janssen says, like someone watching fireworks on the Fourth of July.

Almost everybody else is in the bunker, sitting in the sand. Several people adjust their coats, fastening the Velcro, trying to close any openings in case Iraq fires a Scud loaded with anthrax or a nerve-gas agent.

"Everybody take some naps," somebody says over the radio. "We could be here awhile."

Two missiles shoot into the sky.

Janssen stays outside. He's watching history unfold through his gas mask, and he can't help but look. A former high school football player, Janssen is 5 feet 11 with brown hair and brown eyes. He joined the Marines for the experience, to see different places and things.

This tops everything.

It's surreal, hiding in a bunker, at the start of a war, as your emotions range from panic and fear to relief and boredom, just wanting to take off the gas mask.

Janssen's not a thrill-seeker: "I don't like roller coasters," he says. "They scare the crap out of me."

Janssen, a Marine reservist, hears planes high overhead, but they are out of sight. He holds an M16 rifle in his right hand and leans against the roof with his left. Janssen, 20, is a sophomore at Illinois State University. He plans to major in pre-law or criminal justice, but hasn't decided.

More airplanes go by, and it's obvious they are headed to Iraq to drop bombs.

"You know what's really messed up?" Janssen says to two Marines near him. "There are people dying right now."

There is another explosion behind the bunker.

Everyone assumes it's a Scud that reached the ground. And everybody is thinking the same thing: Where will the next one land?

Cpl. Joe (Goose) Gossmeyer

April 7, 2003

NAME: Joe (Goose) Gossmeyer
RANK: Marine corporal
AGE: 23
HOMETOWN: Stanford, Ill.
DUTY: Driver,
6th Engineer Support Battalion

NAME: Scott Albritton
RANK: Marine corporal
AGE: 25
HOMETOWN: Peoria, Ill.
DUTY: Driver,
6th Engineer Support Battalion

NAME: Garrick Tracy
RANK: Marine corporal
AGE: 24
HOMETOWN: Laura, Ill.
DUTY: Driver,
6th Engineer Support Battalion

Left-behind Marine's death a puzzle

CAMP VIPER, southern Iraq — Was he conscious? Did he see the convoy leaving? Or did he just slip away and die right there in the Iraqi desert?

Sgt. Fernando Padilla Ramirez was left behind in enemy territory when a Marine supply convoy was ambushed north of Nasiriyah, Iraq. Marines didn't know whether Ramirez was dead or alive when the convoy took off without him. His body was recovered a few days later and identified April 10.

"The Iraqis didn't kill him," says Cpl. Scott Albritton, who drove a truck through the ambush. "I think we killed him because we left him behind."

Despite the high-tech weapons that were showcased during the Iraqi war — unmanned drones that patrolled the sky and laser-guided bombs that could find tanks under bridges — Padilla Ramirez's death highlights the low-tech vulnerability of the supply chain. Despite being ordered to drive in blackout conditions, some drivers on the convoy didn't have night-vision goggles, their blackout headlights didn't work, and they didn't have any form of communication.

The military investigation into Padilla Ramirez's death could last months. Officials were unable or unwilling to answer many basic questions about that night.

"How can you leave a guy behind?" asks Cpl. Joe (Goose) Gossmeyer, who also was on the convoy. "I think it's a lack of leadership, a lack of accountability. I don't understand how you leave a Marine behind like that. I can't imagine being that Marine. What if he's conscious and he's watching his convoy leaving?"

So many questions remain, but this much is known about the night it started raining hell, at least from the viewpoint of some of the Marines who were there.

DRIVING NORTH THROUGH IRAQ, Albritton looks out the window at a small town and wonders where all the children have gone.

"It's like a ghost town," he says.

It is March 28, and Albritton is in the passenger seat in a Logistics Vehicle System truck, hauling a tractor and a container full of diesel fuel. He is in the middle of a massive convoy that includes 200 vehicles and stretches about 2 miles long, he says.

The trucks are hauling heavy equipment and supplies, traveling north on Route 7, a major supply route through Iraq.

Albritton, 25, of Peoria, Ill., looks to his right and sees a series of two-story buildings in a town so small he doesn't know its name. He hears a couple of pops and sees a series of flashes, like somebody is taking pictures from a building nearly 220 yards away.

"Is somebody shooting at us?" he wonders.

In the truck ahead of Albritton, Cpl. Garrick Tracy drives an LVS, hauling two bulldozers on a 40-foot trailer. He hears rounds ping off the bulldozers.

Tracy, 24, of Laura, Ill., grabs his M16 rifle and starts to fire.

Ping. Ping.

The bullets keep striking the bulldozers.

About three or four trucks ahead of Tracy, Gossmeyer drives an LVS, pulling heavy equipment. He hears something different: Thump. Thump.

"They're shooting mortar rounds at us," he says. Gossmeyer, 23, of Stanford, Ill., prepares to hit the accelerator.

In a preconvoy meeting, all three were told that if they encounter an ambush, they should punch through it as fast as possible. In a heavy-duty truck, especially an LVS, there is almost no protection — only the speed they can muster.

But the convoy comes to a stop — "right in the middle of the kill zone," Tracy says.

Tracy starts to fire.

Ping. Ping.

Albritton, a Marine reservist who is a salesman for a construction supply company in Bloomington,

Cpl. Garrick Tracy

GARRICK TRACY

April 7, 2003

Ill., leans out his window, points his M16 and tries to find somebody to shoot.

The convoy is guarded by Light Armored Vehicles, which look like tanks but have eight wheels. The LAVs start firing at the buildings. "They were sending hell on it," Albritton says. "I don't know how long we sat there, but it seemed like forever."

Gossmeyer, a Marine reservist who is a police officer in Normal, Ill., estimates they were stopped in the kill zone for about 15 minutes.

"I was scared," Gossmeyer says.

He has never faced fire or shot his weapon as a police officer.

"We were just taking rounds, sitting there," he says. "There's nothing I could do except just sit there and hope I didn't get hit."

Finally, the convoy starts to move again, but it doesn't head out of town into the desert. Instead, the convoy passes through town, does a U-turn on the north end and comes back.

Right through the ambush a second time.

"When we started turning around, I couldn't believe it," Albritton says.

Tracy concentrates on driving as fast as he can.

"I knew all I had to do was keep driving, and I'd be safe," Tracy says. "At the same time, I was scared crapless. I've got a wife and 3-year-old daughter back home. That's the only thing that was going through my mind right then, getting through there safely."

Tracy and his wife, Mindy, have been married for five years and have a daughter, Madeline.

"I was picturing them, the last time I saw them, at the airport leaving Peoria," Tracy says. "They were waving flags and saying, 'I love you.' "

Ping. Ping.

The bullets keep hitting Tracy's vehicle and the tractors. Sitting behind the wheel, he has almost no protection.

"You just lean back as far as you can, hide behind the frame and hold the accelerator to the floor."

The convoy passes through the town and heads toward Nasiriyah. The Marines regroup, eat, fuel up and get ready to go back through the town a third time.

"We checked over our loads and got ready to do it again," Tracy says.

TRACY DOESN'T HAVE night-vision goggles or contact with any other drivers. But he feels safe because he's tucked into the middle of the convoy.

His LVS is a big, lumbering truck with almost no ability to accelerate when pulling heavy equipment. He estimates that it goes from zero to 60 m.p.h. in about 1½ minutes.

As the convoy races to go through the ambush a third time, faster trucks pull away, and the convoy splits, like a snake that has been cut in half.

About 2 miles from the city, Tracy is suddenly out in front. He is the lead vehicle for the second half of the convoy, but he can't see the road. His blackout headlights don't work.

"We are driving blind," he says.

He's not sure where he's going. Are they supposed to go through the middle of the town again? Or take another route?

As he approaches the town, he sees muzzle flashes and green tracer rounds going off.

"You hear mortars everywhere," he says. "They had moved up closer, and they were on both sides of the road, shooting at us. We were just punching through it, hauling ass."

His truck has two blown-out tires, but he doesn't stop.

Cobra helicopters fire at the buildings. His vision improves because buildings and cars are on fire, lighting the road.

"There were blown-up semis and buses in the road," Tracy says. "It was like a slalom course going

Cpl. Scott Albritton

SCOTT ALBRITTON

April 7, 2003

through there. I was running off the road left and right."

Albritton is in the truck, right behind Tracy. The third trip through the city feels worse than the other two.

"It's like messing with a beehive," Albritton says. "All the bees come out of the city."

AFTER PUNCHING THROUGH the town, they drive about 30 miles and then stop at a clearing near a farmhouse.

"When I got out of my truck, I was shaking," Tracy says. He remembers being drenched with sweat. "I was pretty soaked. I had to wash my shirts."

After a moment of relaxation, they hear fire again.

"The guys said they could see enemy in the tree line, shooting mortar rounds," Gossmeyer says. "So they opened fire on them. This one car rolled up, kinda slow. It crept up and stopped, crept up again, stopped and then punched it. The order was given, if it got closer, we had to open up on it. We fired on that pretty good."

After a 1½-hour rest, everybody packs up to leave. As the convoy starts to move, Gossmeyer sees something surprising.

"We were leaving, and for some reason there was a guy in the road," he says.

Gossmeyer picks him up.

"The guy in the road said, 'Hey, they left me. I'm gonna hop a ride with you.'"

Gossmeyer is shocked to see someone left behind. Marines don't leave anyone behind.

THE NEXT DAY, a warrant officer tells the drivers that a sergeant was lost on the convoy.

"The truck overturned," Gossmeyer remembers being told by the warrant officer. "The driver broke his arm. The gunner who was in there got picked up,

but for some reason, the A driver got left behind. It was a sergeant from 371."

There are countless rumors about what happened. Some think a rocket-propelled grenade hit the truck. Others think the truck was driven off the road and two Marines got out and hopped a ride with somebody else. Padilla Ramirez wasn't with them.

THE BODY OF PADILLA RAMIREZ was recovered sometime between April 1 and April 3. Padilla Ramirez of San Luis, Ariz., was a member of the Marine Wing Support Squadron 371. He was 26.

His remains were identified April 10.

"I don't have an exact day" when the body was recovered, says Maj. T.V. Johnson, director of public affairs for the 3rd Marine Aircraft Wing. "I believe they recovered remains they thought were his. The remains had his uniform on it, had his name tag, but because of things that had taken place, they couldn't say, 'Yes, that's him,' even though he was wearing his uniform."

Johnson would not disclose whether Padilla Ramirez died from a crash or was captured and killed.

"It's still under investigation," Johnson says. "It wouldn't be fair to say what's his cause of death."

Padilla Ramirez, who was a motor transport operator, will be awarded a Purple Heart.

"Apparently, the kids he was driving with, they all tumbled out of the vehicle, or they got separated from the vehicle," Johnson says. "They regrouped, joined up with another vehicle. Then, they said, 'Hey, we got somebody missing.' They scoured as best they could. There were no signs. It's just sad."

When the Marines left Padilla Ramirez behind, they didn't know whether he was dead or alive.

"All they knew is that they couldn't find him," Johnson says. "If they found him, they would have drug him along, whether he was unconscious or whatever."

Johnson did not know what type of vehicle Padilla Ramirez was traveling in or the name of the small town where the incident occurred. He would not disclose who was traveling with Padilla Ramirez in the truck or who made the decision to leave him behind.

"The senior man would be the individual responsible for accounting for all of his personnel," Johnson says. "Is someone going to go to jail for it or be punished? It's not a matter of a legal thing. It's something that is ingrained in us. Hey, you bring them back.

"The guy on the scene has to make that call. ... It's a matter of: Did he do everything he could possibly do to recover the remains or recover a Marine alive? Did he knowingly leave someone?"

Johnson also would not explain why the convoy turned around and went through the ambush three times.

"Anything dealing with the mechanics — why they did this — will not be talked about in the open press until the investigation is finalized," Johnson says. "I feel sorry for the families. I feel sorry for the guys who worked closely with the guys on the vehicles that night. I know they are kicking themselves, asking, 'Is there something I could have done?' The answer is probably no. They probably did everything they could. We were fortunate to get out and live to tell about it."

THE EXPERIENCE HAS CHANGED everything for Tracy, Gossmeyer and Albritton.

Starting that night, Tracy was on three different convoys that faced fire in a 12-day period.

"It's pretty scary as a driver," he says. "All you have is speed and your truck. It's just luck of the

April 7, 2003

Cpl. Joe (Goose) Gossmeyer

draw, where they are shooting at."

Tracy, a Marine reservist, works for a plant in Peoria that makes dog food bags.

"We came over here thinking that we aren't going to see anything," Tracy says. "When you see stuff like that, it makes you rethink a whole lot of things."

Even though he is part of the supply chain, Gossmeyer has seen enough combat to realize he was in serious danger.

"I used to think when I get home," he says. "Now, I think if I get home. After you take firefights, you just don't know. When you are driving, it's out of your hands. You might say a little prayer when the convoy takes off. I don't know what's in store for me."

That night changed Albritton's view of Iraqi civilians. It is common for truck drivers to see children by the side of the road, waving to them. But now, he is wary of them: "It could be their parents shooting at you later that night."

KORTUMS, JAMES
MEMORIAL SERVICE

March 30, 2003

CHAPTER 5

A Death in the Family: 'I don't have any answers.'

March 25, 2003

NAME: Timothy Edwards
RANK: Marine lance corporal
AGE: 24
HOMETOWN: Fremont, Wis.
DUTY: Truck driver, Charlie Company,
6th Engineer Support Battalion

Search for comrades an emotional journey

CAMP VIPER, southern Iraq — About 100 Marines gather in a circle, sitting in the sand. Maj. Michael McCarthy walks into the middle of Charlie Company to deliver the news. How do you explain how a Marine can drown in the desert in the middle of a sandstorm?

"We lost two Marines today," he says. "It happened about 12 o'clock or 12:15 this afternoon — Cpl. Evan James and Sgt. Bradley S. Korthaus."

Both Marines — James, 21, of Edwardsville, Ill., and Korthaus, 28, of Davenport, Iowa — were members of Charlie Company, 6th Engineer Support Battalion, which is supplying fuel and water to the 1st Marine Expeditionary Force.

The two Marines drowned while swimming across a 225-foot-wide canal during a reconnaissance mission. Three other Marines made it across safely. All of the Marines were wearing about 30 pounds of gear, including tactical vests and boots. They carried ammunition and M16 rifles.

The Marines were working on the south side of the canal. All day long, there were civilians on the north side of the canal — triggering security concerns about Iraqi militiamen disguising themselves as civilians.

James made it nearly all the way across; he disappeared about 5 feet from shore. Korthaus was last seen about halfway across the canal.

"The water is very cold," McCarthy tells Charlie Company. "I went into the water myself to try to find them."

The search went on for hours.

"We haven't recovered the bodies yet," McCarthy says.

"For those of you who need to see the chaplain, get on the list," McCarthy says. "We grieve our losses. We pick up and move on. I don't have any answers.

"We will find their bodies."

McCarthy's shoulders are slumped; his voice is drained. Usually a calm man, filled with strength, he looks completely exhausted.

"Grief. Sadness. Anger. It's all natural," he says. "Don't be afraid to show your emotions. If you have to do it in private, do it in private. I've cried two times already. They were good Marines, no question about it. They were good men."

Lance Cpl. Timmy Edwards, a youth minister from Wisconsin Rapids, Wis., is called into the center of the group.

Edwards, 24, wants to become a pastor. His nickname, Preacher, is written on the side of his Kevlar helmet.

"On this occasion, everybody can take off their Kevlar," says Edwards. The Marines remove their helmets. "Dear Lord, we come to a sad moment. We mourn and grieve the loss of two great Marines."

For several minutes, he speaks eloquently about the passage from one life to another life. Several Marines are sniffling.

A few hours later, McCarthy returns to the canal along with a security detail and several officers, watching from the sandy shore as a Navy diving team searches the bottom of the canal.

After two days, they find the bodies. McCarthy goes into the ambulance and has to identify James.

"It was one of the hardest things to do," he says, wiping his eyes.

Then, he finds strength.

"We have to get past this," he says. "We have to pick up and move on, or we'll have even more casualties."

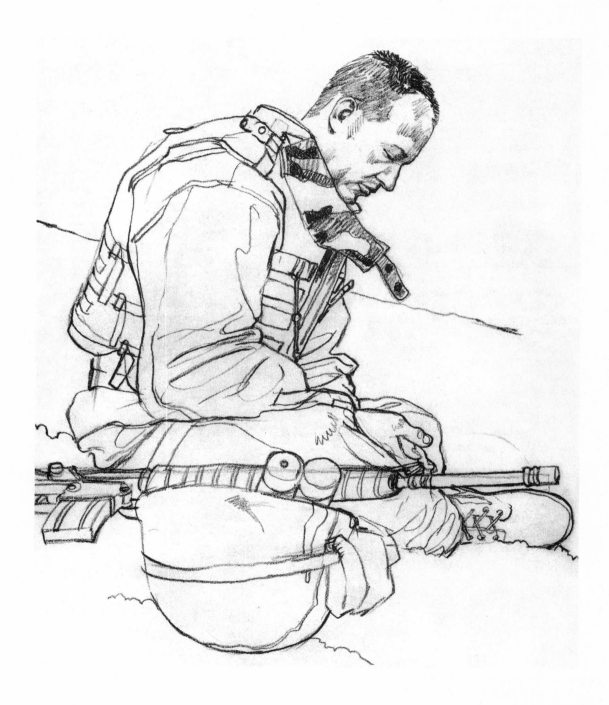

March 26, 2003

NAME: Sgt. Jason Barringer
RANK: Marine sergeant
AGE: 29
HOMETOWN: Decatur, Ill.
DUTY: In charge of platoon of 42 Marines, Charlie Company, 6th Engineer Support Battalion

Marine vows to deliver his pal's good-bye

CAMP VIPER, southern Iraq — Marines call it a death letter, one last chance to say good-bye.

About two weeks ago, Sgt. Bradley Korthaus wrote a letter to his parents. He finished it when he was based at Camp Solomon Islands in Kuwait, preparing to go to war in Iraq. He showed the letter to Sgt. Jason Barringer, a close friend, and gave him specific instructions. "If anything happens to me, you have to promise to mail it," Korthaus said.

Korthaus put the letter in his backpack, in a hidden pocket with a Velcro fastener.

Then, he prodded Barringer to write one, too.

Barringer refused. He was too cocky, too sure of himself. He didn't plan on dying. And he certainly didn't have time to think about it.

"I'm carpe diem," Barringer said.

Live for the moment. No time to think about the future.

But it made Barringer think.

Two weeks later, Barringer is standing watch, near a canal in southern Iraq, when he hears a call for help over the radio.

Korthaus and Cpl. Evan James have disappeared on a reconnaissance mission, while trying to swim across a 225-foot-wide canal to check out some civilians they feared were Iraqi military in disguise.

Barringer runs 700 yards to the shore, strips off his clothes, jumps into the cold water and tries to find the two Marines. Korthaus and James were wearing boots, camouflage clothing, vests and ammunition, and carrying their M16 rifles.

He searches for 30 minutes in the dark, brackish water. He can't see anything, so he tries to feel with his hands. James was a fitness buff, a triathlete and a strong swimmer. Korthaus was a large man, 5 feet 10 and about 210 pounds. "There is almost no current, so they can't go far," Barringer thinks.

Barringer and Korthaus had known each other for about nine years. When Barringer became a pla-

toon sergeant for a reserve unit based in Peoria, Ill., he chose Korthaus to be the assistant squad leader. They roomed together during drill weekends and became good friends. Drinking buddies. Korthaus was a storyteller, funny as heck.

Barringer was in charge of both Korthaus and James. He feels responsible for all of his men. To protect them. To bring them home alive.

Barringer swims across the canal and holds the safety line as five Marines go into the water. He helps organize security and informs the command back at base camp.

Korthaus was a strong-willed man, a plumber by trade, and good with a hammer, Barringer remembers. When they were still in Kuwait, before the war, the 6th Engineer Support Battalion held a Battalion Field Meet on St. Patrick's Day, in honor of the patron saint of engineers. Charlie Company is made up of combat engineers.

Korthaus competed in the nail-driving contest on a five-man team. His team had to pound five nails, about 6 inches long, as fast as possible.

He nailed the first two just fine. Then, he smashed his left thumb. It was bloody and mangled, but he kept working, nailing the other two in no time, helping Charlie Company win the field meet. The prize was nearly priceless: The entire company got three hours of shower time, at a time when there were water restrictions. Everybody else had to take Navy showers, using water only to rinse.

Before Charlie Company left Solomon Islands and headed for Iraq, Korthaus turned to Barringer and they shook hands.

"No matter what happens, it's been great doing this with you," Korthaus said to Barringer.

And now, the clock is ticking. Somebody on shore shouts out the time the two Marines have been underwater: 4 minutes, 15 minutes, 30 minutes, 1 hour.

Eventually, they call off the search.

After three hours, Barringer remembers the letter. He opens Korthaus' pack and finds it already addressed.

Barringer wants to deliver the letter in person, and more than anything, he wants to attend the funeral, but he knows he'll be in Iraq.

For the rest of the night, Barringer keeps a vigil, sitting on the bank of the canal, as Navy divers search for the two Marines.

He doesn't say much, just sits there, staring at the water. But the divers can't find anything.

The next day, Barringer is back on the bank. The wind kicks up a vicious sandstorm. It hurts to be outside. The sand gets in your eyes and teeth, and it pelts your skin. Barringer puts on his goggles and uses a mask to breathe. But he stays on the bank, curled up, trying to stay low.

About 24 hours after the two Marines disappeared, the divers find James. Barringer tells his squad to carry the body to the ambulance.

On Wednesday morning, nearly 48 hours after he disappeared, the divers find Korthaus.

"I'll mail the letter to Korthaus' parents first chance," Barringer says.

He stuffs it into his backpack, in a secure pocket. Right next to the one he wrote for himself.

NAME: James Shields
RANK: Navy petty officer 2nd class
AGE: 23
HOMETOWN: Tolone, Ill.
DUTY: Diver, Underwater Construction Team 2

'We couldn't save the Marines'

CAMP VIPER, southern Iraq — Petty Officer 2nd Class James Shields steps into a Zodiac inflatable boat, wearing a black wet suit. He glances at the dark, choppy water where two Marines disappeared about eight hours ago, during a reconnaissance mission to check on a group of Iraqi civilians.

Sgt. Bradley Korthaus and Cpl. Evan James disappeared while swimming across a 225-foot-wide canal. They are presumed dead.

James disappeared about 5 feet from the north shore. Korthaus went down about halfway.

Now, a Navy diving team is being sent out to look for the bodies in the cold, brackish water.

Shields, 23, who lives in Tolone, Ill., is the backup diver in the Zodiac. If there is an emergency, he'll go into the water.

Five Marines are posted on the north shore, providing security. Maj. Michael McCarthy is on the south shore with several of the commanders from his staff. They wait for hours, sitting on the banks.

The divers work until they run out of air, but they can't find anything. They decide to put up tents and call it a night.

"It was a little scary because of the reason they died," Shields says.

The Marines died trying to secure the far side of the canal. But Shields is afraid it's not safe.

"It was the worst situation to be diving in. It made me nervous."

AT SUNRISE, Shields prepares to go into the water. He eats an MRE for breakfast, starting with the cheese spread, then a chocolate bar.

He's never searched for a body, and the truth is, he's scared. He joined the Navy as a Seabee, which is essentially a construction worker. After two years, he signed up to become an underwater Seabee diver. They inspect bridges and piers and do underwater salvage.

In Iraq, the Navy diving teams are helping build military bridges over rivers.

Shields walks to the water, carrying a cup of coffee and wearing a wet suit and dark Oakley sunglasses.

He peels down his top, and his body is covered with tattoos: a tribal sun on his back, two sharks on his right calf, a tiger on his right shoulder and a Seabee tattoo on his left shoulder.

"Where are we gonna start?" Shields asks.

"We'll show you the spot," says Senior Chief John Green, 41, a master diver from Alliance, Ohio.

Five Marines are posted on the north shore, armed with M16 rifles. Thirteen camels walk by them.

Several Marines sit on the south shore, staring at the water.

The sky is blue, but a sandstorm is kicking up.

"Get in the water," Green says. He likes to let the young divers go first, for experience.

Green tries to explain how they will search under the water, drawing the pattern in the sand on the bank.

"It's gonna take a little time," Green tells a Marine. "But we will find them. We will look until somebody tells us to stop looking. The only way we will have trouble is if the body floated up and the current took them."

The water is about 60 degrees. There are waves on the top of the water, but there is no current near the bottom.

The wind, which never seems to stop in Iraq, goes from strong to nasty. Now, it's a full-blown sandstorm.

Shields scoots into the water and begins to work. It is tedious, repetitive work, sweeping back and forth with his hands, unable to see because the water is so murky.

On the north shore, a Marine reports that someone dressed like a shepherd is about 300 meters

Navy Petty Officer 2nd Class James Shields waits to enter the water to search for the bodies of two missing Marines.

March 26, 2003

away from him and closing.

"Keep your eye on the shepherd," the Marine is told.

Three mangy dogs approach the Marines on the south shore, but the Marines chase them away.

After 65 minutes, Shields pops up.

"Does he have something?" Green asks.

No.

He's out of air.

"It was a mess," Shields says. "It was murky as heck, but you do whatever it takes."

Another diver goes into the water.

And then another.

They search for hours.

The sandstorm grows in strength, one of the worst in two months. Waves crest at 2 feet. The boat bobs in the canal. And soon, you can't see the boat from shore. The sand stings your face and peppers your hands. Everyone is caked sandy brown.

The Marines sit on shore, their faces wrapped with cloth, just so they can breathe. Finally, at about 1 p.m., after they've been at work for about five hours, a diver finds James. The divers are excited, but they don't share it, trying to be respectful.

The Marines carry the body to an ambulance.

The divers go back to work.

At about 6 p.m., the weather is so bad Green can't see his divers in the water. He feels it's too unsafe, and he calls off the search, vowing to get back to work at the crack of dawn. "We can't leave," he says.

Shields goes to his tent near the shore. "The weather was nasty," he says. "The water was all messed up."

The next day, the divers return to the water. They find Korthaus and put him into an ambulance and return to base camp.

"Obviously, we couldn't save the Marines," Green says. "This was for the families."

.

KORTUHS, JAMES
MEMORIAL SERVICE

NAME: Bradley Korthaus
RANK: Marine sergeant
AGE: 28
HOMETOWN: Davenport, Iowa
DUTY: Combat engineer, Charlie Company,
6th Engineer Support Battalion

NAME: Evan James
RANK: Marine corporal
AGE: 21
HOMETOWN: Edwardsville, Ill.
DUTY: Combat engineer, Charlie Company,
6th Engineer Support Battalion

Two rifles, two helmets — one memorial in the sand

CAMP VIPER, southern Iraq — Two M16 rifles are stuck in the sand, upside down, by the edge of the water.

Following Marine Corps tradition, the helmets of Sgt. Bradley Korthaus and Cpl. Evan James are placed on their rifles, about 10 feet from the canal where they died.

"Marines, thanks for coming down," Maj. Michael McCarthy says Sunday afternoon, starting the memorial service. "Give us your prayers."

Korthaus and James drowned March 24 while trying to swim across a 225-foot-wide canal during a reconnaissance mission.

"We are here to give honor to their lives and to speak well of their sacrifice," the Rev. Ben Orchard says, giving the invocation. He hands out bulletins with a color picture of the Iwo Jima War Memorial, which he brought to Iraq just in case there was a tragedy.

About 100 Marines from the 6th Engineer Support Battalion gather in a semicircle, by the bank of the canal. Lance Cpl. Matthew Dickson holds the Marine Corps flag, which sways slowly in the light, steady wind. The Marines are told to take off their Kevlar helmets.

"They lived their lives as Marines, and that's the highest compliment I can give," says Lt. Col. Roger Machut, who is in charge of the battalion.

Sgt. Jason Barringer stands up. After diving into the water and trying to save them, he kept vigil by the water for two days until both bodies were found.

"I was extremely good friends with Korthaus," Barringer says. "He really gave of himself. He was a storyteller. I lost a very good friend. And Corporal James was becoming a fine" noncommissioned officer. "I hate the fact that I'm not going to see him lead Marines. I'm going to miss him."

He chokes back tears and sits down.

Cpl. Joel Graves was swimming next to James when he went down, not far from the bank.

"James was an outstanding triathlete," Graves says. "When we were swimming, we were very close, right next to each other. When he started to go down, he could have pulled me down with him. He knew, if he had grabbed at me, I would have drowned."

It is a surreal scene. As the Marines sing "Amazing Grace" in a country they invaded less than two weeks ago, several armed guards are posted around the area for security.

On the other side of the canal, three camels walk along the bank.

Earlier in the day, Marines met with investigators looking into the incident. Right after the drownings, the focus was on recovering the bodies and dealing with the loss. Weeks later, some Marines would openly question why the two were sent across the canal.

After the service, Brig. Gen. Edward Usher speaks to Charlie Company.

"I didn't know these Marines," Usher says. "But I know the effort and work of Charlie Company. This mission has been a success because of you and them. You'll be successful no matter what.

"I don't know if you had a guardian angel before, but now you have two in heaven. Keep focused. And if you fall, you'll have two angels to greet you."

Sgt. Maj. Manuel Sanchez steps into the middle of the group and says, "From now on, the two pointer stars in the Big Dipper will symbolize Korthaus and James for the members of Charlie Company. When I look at it. I will think of them."

Nine Marines walk to the water and kneel in the sand, as if at an altar. Four Marines sit in front of the M16 rifles, staring at the helmets.

The flag continues to sway, ever so slightly, in the gentle breeze.

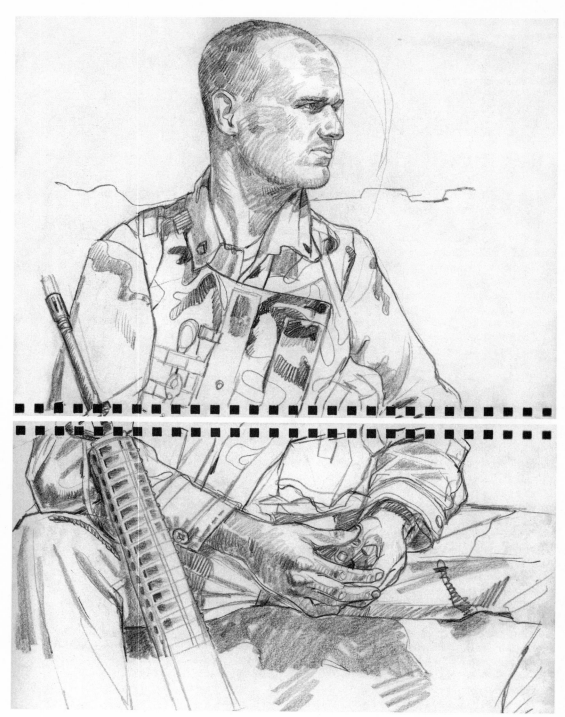

April 13, 2003

CHAPTER 6

Sacrifice: 'I'm missing a lot of my family's life.'

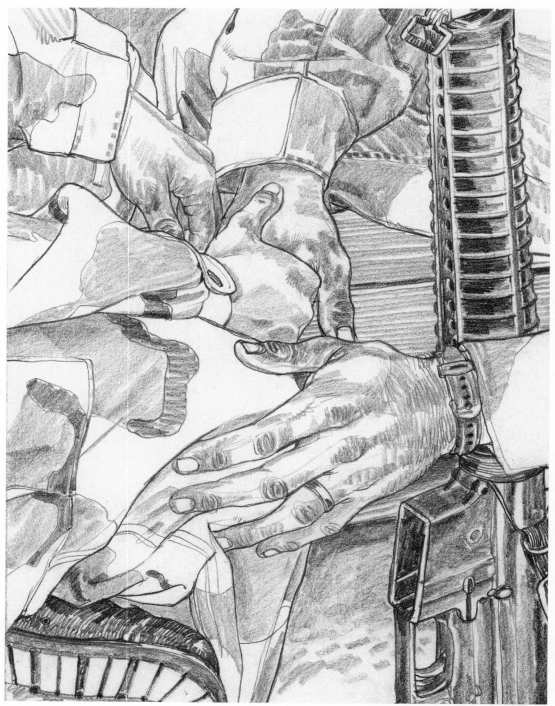

March 12, 2003

NAME: Erica Gonzales
RANK: Marine lance corporal
AGE: 20
HOMETOWN: Phoenix, Ariz.
DUTY: Bulk fuel specialist, Charlie Company,
6th Engineer Support Battalion

NAME: Alejandro Gonzales
RANK: Navy petty officer 2nd class
AGE: 20
HOMETOWN: Phoenix
DUTY: Construction worker
6th Engineer Support Battalion

March 12, 2003

Rendezvous is short on romance

CAMP SOLOMON ISLANDS, Kuwait — Navy Petty Officer 2nd Class Alejandro Gonzales sits on a bench outside his wife's tent with his hat pulled down low, so he doesn't spoil the surprise.

"Hey, I need to talk to you," Sgt. Raul Amezcu says to Marine Lance Cpl. Erica Gonzales in a stern voice.

Erica walks with him, thinking she's in trouble, but she can't figure it out.

"Oh man, what did I do?" she thinks.

She walks across the gravel, wearing fatigues, helmet and flak jacket, and carrying her M16. She doesn't notice the man in fatigues. She hasn't seen her husband in more than two months. She's in the Marines. He's in the Navy. They are both stationed in Kuwait, but she hasn't been able to find him.

He spots the boots first, Marine issue, tiny size 4's. He gets up and walks toward her. For a split second, she doesn't recognize him. His hair is longer. His face is thinner.

"Erica," he says.

She tries to be strong, tries to be a tough Marine, but she starts to cry. She has always been sensitive, so shy she'd skip school to avoid people, and that's why she joined the Marine Reserve. To gain self-con-

March 12, 2003

fidence. She still doesn't know if she can kill somebody.

He kisses her on the cheek. Can a Marine hug a
sailor? Even if they are married?

"I've never drilled for this," she thinks.

They hug and sit on the bench, about 2 feet apart.

Alejandro is a construction worker, based at
Camp Fox, south of Camp Solomon Islands. When he
came north for bridge training, he asked a lieutenant
colonel if he knew the location of the 6th Engineer
Support Battalion.

"Right there," he said. After one boss talked to
another boss, Alejandro was allowed to go visit his
wife.

For two hours.

"I can't believe you're here," she says, grabbing
his shoulders.

He looks around the base. He says Camp Solomon
Islands looks just like his base.

"That's our chow hall," she says, pointing at a
large white tent.

"We have a galley tent, just like it," he says.

A fly lands on his rifle, and she brushes it away.

"We get ice cream," she says.

"We don't get ice cream," he says. "But we get
meals shipped in. For lunch, we get a cold sandwich."

"What?" she asks. "We get MREs."

"But they suck," he says. "They are like tuna, but
it's like eating rocks and sand."

THEY'VE KNOWN EACH OTHER since they were
in Junior ROTC at Westview High School in Phoenix,
Ariz. They've been married just over a year and want
to start a family.

"We get bottled water," she says.

"Yeah, we get bottled water," he says.

"Do you have phones?" she asks.

"No. Do you?"

"No."

"I mailed you a letter last night," she says.

"I'll probably get it by the time the war is over,"
he says.

They sit facing each other. At first, they don't
touch. But they slide closer.

She puts her helmet at her side. She has written
his name on her helmet and her goggles. Deeply religious, she has drawn three crosses on her helmet,
above her forehead.

"My platoon gave me this nickname," she says.
"They call me Little Foot."

Her pants are baggy. She has lost about 8 pounds,
and her belt is 2 inches too big. But she hasn't gotten
sick.

"The first week we were here, there were 110 cases of strep throat," she says.

After 20 minutes, they are locked eye to eye, his
left hand on her right knee.

"Our whole battalion is reserves," she says.

"Yeah," he says. "I know."

"Every night at 8 o'clock, they show a movie in the
chow hall," she says.

"We barely got a TV," he says. "They have American DVDs and an Arabic DVD player and the cod-
ing is different, so we can't use it."

There is silence.

"I don't know what else to say," she says.

"Me, neither."

It's awkward and strange, like a weird first date for
a couple who've been married for more than a year.

"Sure enough, here we are," he says, for the third
time.

She points across camp.

"I built one of these bunkers," she says.

"I dug one by hand," he says.

He tells her that he keeps a picture of her in his
Bible, so when he wants to see her, it reminds him to
study the scripture.

She does the same thing.

March 12, 2003

She tells him she sleeps on the ground, in a sleeping bag.

He says he doesn't have a pillow.

"I use my Kevlar, and I use the suspension system as a pillow," he says. "The racks suck. You are in your sleeping bags, and if you roll, you fall out. We had a kid fall out. He had a nightmare. The second night we were there. We hear, 'No! No! No!' I guess he was having a nightmare, right? Then, he kicks out, 'cause he was in the bag and he slid. His face was nasty. Blood all over the place. We were like, 'Dude, are you all right?' He says, 'I'm all right; my shoulder hurts.'

"He was all bleeding everywhere. It was nasty."

She tries to top it with an injury story of her own: "A guy was going on a field operation and he had to get on a 7-ton, and he missed the step and he hit the bridge of his nose on the door and he had to get stitches."

"Oooh," he groans.

THE TWO HOURS FLY BY, but now it's over.

As they walk across the base, she looks at him.

"You might want to wear your helmet," she says.

It's a rule at Camp Solomon Islands. Everybody has to wear a helmet.

She wants to hold his hand, but she hesitates. She assumes it's against regulations. Marines march by in unison. A helicopter flies in the distance. At the far side of the camp, by a sand berm, he subtly grabs her hand, but she's afraid. She slides away and holds his canteen.

Four guys run by, doing daily physical training, carrying gas masks.

Erica and Alejandro arrive at the meeting point, but they are early.

They show each other their knives. He just got a new one. She points at her bayonet.

"I used this knife opening a box," she says. "I did better with my fingers."

Trucks go by, kicking up dust.

"I dropped my toothbrush right in the dirt, and I had to throw it away," he says.

"Do you have another?"

"Yeah, I got two extra. Do you have enough?"

"I only have one," she says. "I need a toothbrush case. I'm using a plastic bag, but it's getting nasty."

"I'll try to get one to you."

They sit and wait, 2 feet apart, both in full gear.

They take sips of water from a hose coming off their CamelBaks, a bladder of water worn on the back.

"Yesterday, we were learning how to handle enemy prisoners of war," she says. "It was fun because I didn't think I could do something like that."

He doesn't know what to think about having his wife fight in a war. He just hopes she doesn't change.

Lt. Col. Kirk Jansen, from Grand Rapids, Mich., pulls up in a white SUV.

"I gotta go," Alejandro says, taking off his M16 to get into the truck.

They hug and hold each other, just out of view of the lieutenant colonel.

Alejandro gets into the backseat.

"Thank you," Erica says to Jansen.

"You bet," he says.

As the white SUV drives away, Erica waves at her husband.

She can't stop smiling.

A few days later, a gunnery sergeant approaches her.

"Do you have a husband, Alejandro, who is a Seabee?" he asks.

She has a horrible feeling. Is this how they tell you if there is an accident?

She thinks he's dead.

Tears run down her face.

"I think this is yours," he says, handing her a toothbrush case.

Feb. 11, 2003

NAME: Sally Curlis (right)
RANK: Army corporal
AGE: 20
HOMETOWN: Omaha, Neb.
DUTY: Humvee team member, Central Command

NAME: Nathaniel Snow
RANK: Army sergeant
AGE: 25
HOMETOWN: Killeen, Texas
DUTY: Leads four-soldier Humvee team, Central Command

Too many assignments to look back

SALLY CURLIS

Feb. 11, 2003

DOHA, Qatar — Sgt. Nathaniel Snow is too busy to look up. He's bent over, working quickly inside the back of a Humvee.

It's easier to stay busy, so he won't think about everything he's missing.

"I missed my son's first birthday, first Christmas and second Valentine's Day," says Snow, 25. "I missed him walking. I missed him getting his first tooth. And I will miss his first words by the time we get back."

His son, Ethan, is almost 13 months old.

Snow has been gone since November. He's stationed at Camp As Sayliyah, where U.S. commanders have set up Central Command, preparing for a possible war in Iraq.

"I call my wife about twice a week," he says.

He gets to talk to his wife, Christina, for about 20 minutes.

Christina puts the phone on Ethan's ear, and the baby babbles.

"It's not really words," says Nathaniel, whose voice has an edge, somewhere between anger and resolve.

"I'm doing this to keep my country safe," he says. "I'm trying to protect it from terrorists, so we don't have to worry. If we can stop it here, we might as well stop it, rather than waiting."

Snow is an Army team leader of a four-person Humvee. He supervises Cpl. Sally Curlis, 20.

Snow and Curlis pack tools and sort parts. It's a dirty, grimy job, but her hands look pristine, her fingernails perfect.

Two weeks ago, she went to a beauty salon on the base and had her nails done with clear polish, and she got highlights in her hair.

Did anyone notice?

"I'm too busy to notice things like that," Snow says.

Without looking up.

Feb. 11, 2003

NAME: Nicholas Nenoff
RANK: Army sergeant
AGE: 21
HOMETOWN: Lansing, Mich.
DUTY: Runs post office, 129th Postal Company

Mail call means special delivery

DOHA, Qatar — The mail arrives every day, and the messages are almost always the same, even for the postman: "I love you. I miss you. Can't wait for you to come home. Big hugs."

Cards. Boxes. Letters.

And the best of all: cookies.

"My wife takes care of me," says Sgt. Nicholas Nenoff of the Army's 129th Postal Company based at Ft. Bragg, N.C. "She sends me something every day, and she makes cookies for me and my guys. You can't beat cookies — that and candy."

Nenoff runs the post office at Camp As Sayliyah, headquarters of U.S. forces if there is a war in Iraq.

He stands in an office full of boxes, letters and bins, holding a plastic container full of crumbs that he just got from his wife, Kari. He scoops up some and eats them.

"There is a secret that most people don't know," Nenoff says. "If you put the cookies in a coffee can, they won't crumble."

His favorite are peanut butter cookies with chocolate Hershey's Kisses.

"I get three or four cookies out of a batch that aren't destroyed by the time they get here, but that's all right with me," he says.

When he joined the Army after graduating from Perry High School near Lansing, he dreamed of doing heroic things.

"This is one place I never saw myself, but everybody has to do a job," he says. "I like this job. Everybody likes you. Everybody makes you feel important, because everybody wants their mail. It feels good. It's a big morale boost."

Nenoff has three bits of advice about mailing things to troops overseas: Pack the boxes tightly, don't send pornography or alcohol, because it will be confiscated, and use Priority Mail. "Standard mail is a little cheaper, but it takes about a month or so," he says. "Priority Mail is about two weeks."

Nenoff guarantees that mail will not be lost if it makes it to his office. But that's not to say that everything in his office is supposed to be there. The other day, Nenoff came across a letter from a civilian in Texas to a civilian in Connecticut.

"It ended up in one of my bags," he says. "I checked, assuming it was returned to sender, but no, it was a normal person mailing to a normal person, and it ended up over here."

He shrugs: "Sometimes, it just happens like that."

This is Nenoff's second deployment in the last 1½ years. He was in Kosovo for seven months before arriving in Qatar.

"My wife is getting used to it," he says.

She sends him two or three e-mails a day.

"E-mails are great," he says, "but nothing lasts like a letter."

March 29, 2003

NAME: Jeremy DeVault
RANK: Marine lance corporal
AGE: 21
HOMETOWN: Chillicothe, Ill.
DUTY: Combat engineer, Charlie Company,
6th Engineer Support Battalion

March 29, 2003

Marines are family in the desert

CAMP CHESTY, central Iraq — For Lance Cpl. Jeremy DeVault, this war has been a grand adventure — wild, frightening, exciting, boring, sad and fun.

"It's been an experience of a lifetime," DeVault says. "It's something you can go back and tell your friends about. Nobody has been to Kuwait or Iraq. Nobody is ever going to come here to visit a country like this."

DeVault, 21, of Chillicothe, Ill., is a combat engineer with Charlie Company, 6th Engineer Support Battalion.

"It's like a big family," DeVault says. "I'll remember how close everybody came together. How everybody was willing to do everything for each other, to be one family."

He's been here so long, the desert is starting to feel like home. He's used to sleeping on the ground and eating prepackaged meals.

A few weeks ago, DeVault was asked to work security for a convoy going south to a camp in Kuwait. He stayed for two days, sleeping on a cot in an air-conditioned tent. He took showers and watched television.

"I felt awkward being down there, when my fellow Marines are up here," he says. "It wasn't bad coming back here. This is home, you know."

DeVault joined the Marines, following in the foot-steps of his father, Kenneth R. DeVault.

"He was in force recon in Vietnam and Korea," DeVault says.

"He wouldn't talk about it too much. He would talk about how the Viet Cong would try to slit their throats during their sleep. Crazy stuff like that. He was hit with grenade shrapnel in his back during a helicopter drop.

"The grenade cut through the bottom part of his backbone. They told him that he would never be able to walk again, and they wanted to cut the nerves to his legs.

"But he was walking within a year. He was an inspiration. He was so proud of himself. He never really imposed himself on me. But you could see the way he carried himself and how it made a differ-ence in his life."

DeVault's father died June 11, 2001, from an infec-tion.

"It was the hardest time in my life," DeVault says. "I think about him all the time. He's always with me because of what he did in his life. I pray for him to help me."

For DeVault, the highlight of the war was on the first day. As he packed to leave Breach Point West, getting ready to join a convoy headed for the Iraqi border, he watched a barrage of artillery go off.

"We were right there," he says. "It was like a movie. It surprised you at first, then you kind of rolled with it. You could see the flashes of lights. You could hear the rounds projecting.

"That's when I said, 'Yeah, we are really here. You really need to get this job done.' "

DeVault, a 6-foot-1 reservist with blond hair and blue eyes, is a student at Illinois Community College in Peoria, studying accounting.

"Eventually, I want to own my own business, either a bar or an apartment complex, something like that."

He doesn't have kids or even a girlfriend, and he's not in a rush to get home.

"I miss friends and family, just being able to do what I want, when I want," he says. "I signed this contract to do a job. You just got to go with the punches."

April 13, 2003

NAME: Jacob Emmons
RANK: Marine private 1st class
AGE: 19
HOMETOWN: Tremont, Ill.
DUTY: Combat engineer, Charlie Company,
6th Engineer Support Battalion

In the desert, Marine dreams of baseball

CAMP CHESTY, central Iraq — Pfc. Jacob Emmons digs into a pile of dirt, building a bunker. Wearing sandy-brown boots, his feet hurt and they feel as if they're bleeding, but it helps to keep working, to keep his mind off the pain.

He digs into the dirt again and smells something familiar, something far away.

"You know what that smells like?" he says, putting his face close to the soil. "It smells like baseball."

For several weeks, Emmons was based at a Marine camp in the middle of the Iraqi desert. There was nothing but sand in every direction. No sign of life, nothing but a big sweeping sky and an occasional sandstorm. Now he has moved forward, to a camp about 80 miles from Baghdad. The dirt is rich, the weather seems 20 degrees cooler, and the horizon is full of life — palm trees and long grass.

"Baseball," he says, and smiles.

Emmons, 19, a Marine Corps reservist from Tremont, Ill., is a combat engineer for Charlie Company, 6th Engineer Support Battalion. He had a baseball scholarship to Spoon River College in Canton, Ill., but he had to turn it down when he was activated.

"I called up the baseball coach, and I told him that I thought we were going to get activated," Emmons says. "He said, 'That's cool. We'll re-up your scholarship for next year.' "

Emmons grew up a Marine brat. He was born at the Guantanamo Bay naval base in Cuba, where his father, Rod Emmons, was stationed.

"I have pictures of me as a kid, sitting on howitzers and on big" artillery, he says. "It was pretty cool. My dad got discharged from the Marines because he hurt his back. I've always heard stories about the Marines, and I wanted to join. My dad said that he didn't want me to join the Marine Corps unless I got an education out of it, too."

So Emmons joined the reserves.

When the United States invaded Iraq, the

April 13, 2003

Marines wore biochemical suits and rubber boots in case Iraq launched a biological or chemical attack. Emmons wore the rubber boots over his leather boots for more than 30 hours straight without changing his socks. His feet were drenched with sweat.

"My feet couldn't breathe," he says. "After that, my feet started hurting a little bit."

A few days later, he noticed a little red patch on his left foot.

"I wasn't going to complain to the corpsman about that," Emmons says. "He would say, 'Just suck it up.' From there, we started working, laying wire,

April 13, 2003

setting up trip flares. We had to work dusk to dawn, every day."

He let his feet air out at night. But he didn't change his socks, and he didn't use any foot powder; all rookie mistakes.

A few days ago, a doctor stopped by Camp Chesty and asked if anybody had any medical problems.

Several Marines took off their boots.

"That's just heat rash," the doctor said to one Marine.

"Oh, those are just calluses," he told another.

Then he looked at Emmons' feet. They were blood red.

"Your feet have got to be killing you," the doc said.

"Yeah, a little bit," he said.

"You know what this is?"

"No."

"Right there, that's swamp foot," the doctor said, pointing at Emmons' heel. Then he motioned to the rest of it.

"That's the start of cellulitis," he said. "I can see it going up your foot."

Emmons got a 10-day course of antibiotics and a big lecture.

"They told me that I'm a private 1st class, and I don't know the tricks of the trade," Emmons says.

He was ordered to wash his feet twice a day, change his socks every chance he gets and use foot powder.

He's been on light duty for the last three days. He sits in a bunker, with his socks off, wearing sandals.

Emmons has been on antibiotics, and his feet are getting better. Now they are pink, purple, red and yellow. But the color seems to be fading, and the pain is almost all gone.

He senses that the war is starting to come to a close, and it makes him think about going home even more.

"On post, there is nothing out there, and you just gaze off and say, 'I wish I was back home playing baseball.'"

April 16, 2003

NAME: Tim Partridge
RANK: Marine staff sergeant
AGE: 32
HOMETOWN: Williamston, Mich.
DUTY: Heavy-equipment operator,
6th Engineer Support Battalion

Prank call turns lives upside down

CAMP IWO JIMA, Kuwait — Michelle Partridge picks up the telephone and hears the message she has been dreading for months, since her husband, Marine Staff Sgt. Tim Partridge, left for Kuwait. "Your husband is missing in action," someone tells her on the phone. "He is presumed dead."

There is no reason to doubt the caller. He seems to know everything about her husband: his name, rank, unit and Social Security number.

Michelle Partridge, a stay-at-home mom with three kids, collapses in panic.

She assumes the worst. She has no idea that it's a sick prank.

Tim Partridge, a Marine Corps reservist from Williamston, Mich., is stationed near Kuwait City, working at a storage camp for the 6th Engineer Support Battalion, far from the action. But she knows there is danger everywhere in the war zone.

She calls her husband's Marine Reserve station in Battle Creek, Mich., and she is told he is fine. They don't know anything about a missing Marine.

Still, she makes more phone calls. Writes more e-mails.

"No," they keep telling her. "We haven't heard anything." If he were really missing, she is told, they would have notified her in person.

And she can't get in touch with her husband.

On Sunday morning in Kuwait, Tim Partridge doesn't know the two days of hell his wife has lived through back in Michigan.

Partridge, a heavy-equipment operator, is stationed at Camp Iwo Jima near Kuwait City.

It's basically a giant storage facility in the desert with extra equipment, wood and supplies.

He is going through his regular routine, unloading and loading gear. When he goes to the office, a captain stops him.

"You need to read this e-mail," the captain says.

The e-mail has bounced across the chain of command and has finally landed in the right spot.

It explains how Partridge's wife received a message that he was missing in action.

Partridge feels helpless, confused.

He calls his wife on a phone that has a direct line to the states.

The call gets through. It's about 3 a.m. Sunday in Michigan when his wife answers.

"Hey," Tim Partridge says. "I hear you got a message."

"Oh, my God," she says. "I can't believe I'm hearing your voice. Thank God, I am hearing your voice."

They talk for about a half-hour.

"It's horrible, and it's a prank," Tim Partridge says. "From talking to my wife, from what I understand, it's happening across the country, in the United States. Somebody is doing this terrible prank to families with loved ones over here."

Tim Partridge has no idea who would do such a thing.

"She said they told her that I was MIA and presumed dead," he says. "If somebody told me that about my wife or my children, I can't imagine how I'd feel. ... I'd hate to meet that guy. ... There are some things you don't put people through. The families are going through enough with their loved ones being over here."

Just a few hours after the phone call, Partridge is back at work, upbeat, directing his Marines.

But it's all an act.

"I try to stay strong, mentally strong and physically strong, for both your families back home, yourself and the Marines around you," Partridge says. "If you show the weaknesses that you have, even though we all have them, everybody else sees them."

With the war entering a new phase, rebuilding the government and fixing the infrastructure, the Marines are starting to think about going home. But Partridge, who has been deployed since Jan. 27, tries to remind his Marines that they could be overseas several more months. The Marines from the 6th Engineer Support Battalion don't expect to get home before October.

"That's the feel, that's the vibe, that it's over," Partridge says.

During the 1991 Persian Gulf War, Partridge was a lance corporal and helped supply fuel for the tankers.

"We took some artillery, nothing major," he says. "I was never worried about the situation. Back then, I wasn't married and didn't have kids. I didn't have the worries that I have now."

Partridge and his wife have been married seven years. They have three children: Kimberly, 5; John, 3, and Nicole, 1.

"I miss them dearly," he says. "I got new pictures today, from all three of them, in an Easter card."

Partridge takes some comfort knowing his wife has a strong support system.

"The mother-in-law lives 1½ miles away," he says. "My father lives a couple of miles the other way. I have a brother who lives right across the street. We are a tight family, and we are really close together. They are really helping her out a lot."

For the last eight years, Partridge has been a member of the Marine Reserve, based in Battle Creek. He works as a heavy-equipment operator for a contractor in Lansing, Mich. But he's starting to sense that his military career might be coming to an end.

"After this, I don't know," he says. "I'm missing a lot of my family's life. I don't like it, and a lot of the Marines don't like it. But we also know that's part of our job as a Marine. We know that's a risk we take when we signed. The reasons we do these wars, and the reasons we fight these wars, I understand them. There are a lot of people who don't."

Even worse, there are people who twist it all into a sick prank joke.

April 8, 2003

NAME: Charmain Jones
RANK: Marine sergeant
AGE: 27
HOMETOWN: Houston, Texas
DUTY: Electrician, 6th Engineer Support Battalion

Kid stuff keeps mom smiling

CAMP VIPER, southern Iraq — Sgt. Charmain Jones is sure about one thing: Her three children are getting spoiled rotten.

Both Jones and her husband, Sgt. Terrance Jones, are Marines stationed in Iraq. Their three children — Demetrice, 4; Michael, 2, and Natasha, 6 months — are staying with their grandparents, Johnny and Melondy Jones, in Bradenton, Fla.

"I don't think they miss me at all," Jones says, smiling. "They are with their grandparents. They are getting away with murder."

Jones, 27, of Houston, Texas, is an electrician with the 6th Engineer Support Battalion. Her husband helps build runways with another unit. They met in the Marines in 1999.

"He's at the Air Force base, like 35 minutes from Camp Coyote," she says. "I saw him once when I was at Coyote. I was happy. We had been separated for a month or a month and a half. I like playing with my kids and my husband. My husband and I are like two big kids."

She has been in Iraq since Feb. 6.

"Am I sick of it?" she says. "It's tolerable, but I can't wait to go home."

Jones joined the Marines seven years ago, for a $2,000 bonus and a chance to go to school.

She is to get out Dec. 2 and says she doesn't plan to reenlist.

This is her third deployment. She has been to Bolivia and Greece.

"I've left my kids before," she says.

She can't wait to see her kids. Her smile grows stronger as she talks about them.

"Demetrice loves her grandpa," Jones says. "And their grandma loves children. I'm sure they are getting spoiled. But they are in good hands.

"Demetrice is sneaky. She tries to get away with everything. And my son, he is rough. He likes to pick with her, to make her mad, just because he knows he can do it. She'll start crying and go and tell my husband and me. My son thinks it's funny, and my husband thinks it's funny."

Her smile fades. As much as she wants to see her children, she's prepared for a rough homecoming.

"I think I'll be heartbroken when I see them," she says. "I know how my daughter was when I left her for the first time for three months. When I came back, she looked at me like, 'Who is this lady, waking me up at 6 o'clock in the morning?' She didn't know who I was. So I kind of expect it."

April 12, 2003

NAME: Tiffany Carlson
RANK: Marine corporal
AGE: 21
HOMETOWN: Vancouver, Wash.
DUTY: Security detail for Lt. Col. Roger Machut,
6th Engineer Support Battalion

Fun is operating a machine gun

ON THE ROAD TO BAGHDAD, central Iraq — Cpl. Tiffany Carlson doesn't want the war to end. She's having too much fun, riding around the desert with a powerful machine gun, sitting on a box of grenades.

"I don't want to go home," Carlson says. "I like it here. I'm having fun."

She volunteered to be part of the personal security team for Lt. Col. Roger Machut, in charge of 6th Engineer Support Battalion. Carlson operates the M240 Gulf machine gun, the biggest weapon on the four-person security team.

"I asked for it," she says. "I wanted a big gun. I just like to fire it."

When Machut travels around Iraq, Carlson rides in a Humvee behind him. She sits on a box of grenades so she can see over the roof. The machine gun is mounted on a tripod, which she slides back and forth on a wooden platform whenever she sees something suspect.

Her shoulder gets bruised after about 100 shots.

"With the tripod on it, it's very accurate," she says. "I get a lot of adrenaline rushes when I think something is going to happen, whenever I see a truck of Iraqis."

Traveling north toward Baghdad, the route is lined with Iraqi children. But Carlson has to keep the gun pointed near them.

"I always aim in," she says. "I got a brief that they could have grenades or stuff like that. I'm at war. I don't want to shoot kids, but I think it's better them than me."

Carlson joined the Marines two years ago because she wanted to do something different after high school.

"I decided to join the Marine Corps," Carlson says. "Plus, I wanted to stay in shape and have a challenge. I wanted to get stuff done." Carlson, a Marine reservist, manages a store in Portland, Ore., and wants to become a dress designer.

April 12, 2003

"I'm thinking I want to go to school as soon as I get back," she says. "I want to design my own clothes." She will go to Clark College in Vancouver, then transfer to the University of Washington.

She's pretty sure she has a boyfriend back home.

"As far as I know, I think I do," she says. "But I haven't gotten a letter, so I have no idea what's going on."

She's getting a new perspective on guys, lately, as the only woman in her squad.

"You learn how to live how guys live," she says. "When I first joined the Marine Corps, it was kind of tough because of the things they say, but now, I'm one of the guys.

"Everybody in my squad is like a family now. We've gotten really close, and I don't want it to end."

April 12, 2003

NAME: John Alvarado
RANK: Marine lance corporal
AGE: 20
HOMETOWN: Peoria, Ill.
DUTY: Combat engineer, Charlie Company,
6th Engineer Support Battalion

A long way from Peoria, Marine reminisces about home

CAMP VIPER, southern Iraq — Lance Cpl. John Alvarado misses french fries and phone calls, beer and tequila.

He misses ordering pizza. "And I don't even like pizza," Alvarado says. "I just wish I had the chance to order some."

He misses waking up and drinking coffee on his porch back home in Peoria, Ill. Alvarado is a combat engineer in Charlie Company, 6th Engineer Support Battalion, which has set up camp in southern Iraq. Out in the desert, he drinks coffee warmed on a makeshift stove — an empty ammunition case filled with diesel fuel and sand. The top is covered with wire. He drinks the coffee out of an aluminum canteen cup while sitting in the sand.

He misses seeing the sun rise over the Illinois River. Alvarado works as a maintenance worker at the Illinois Valley Yacht and Canoe Club. He used to get there an hour early every morning to watch the sun rise. Some of his coworkers recently sent him a care package with baby wipes, cookies and cards.

"It's a tight little family there," Alvarado says.

He misses the smell of a woman's perfume. A few weeks ago, he got a Dear John letter.

"All my letters are Dear John letters," he jokes, "because my name is John; but this was the real thing."

Alvarado dated a girl named Nicole for about three weeks before he left for Kuwait.

"She was so hot, awesome, smoking," he says. "I knew it wasn't going to last. She had an ex-boyfriend, and it was only a matter of time before she went back to him. I got a letter from her that said she really liked me, but she wanted to go back to him. I knew it was coming. I knew she wasn't the one. She was just fun to hang out with for a while."

He misses smoking cigarettes. His stash ran out four days ago, but the people in his squad try to help him out. They smoke one partway down and let him finish it. He normally smokes a pack a day.

"I don't know if it's the habit or the nicotine," he says. "In the Marine Corps, you have a lot of downtime, and it's something to do."

As strange as it might seem, he misses traveling. His mom, Roberta Alvarado, works as a flight attendant for United Airlines, and he gets to fly for free. He's been to Hong Kong, Germany, London and Hawaii. When a Marine recruiter tried to use a sales pitch promoting travel opportunities and offering a chance to see the world, Alvarado laughed and said, "Nah, I get to travel already." But he doesn't feel as if he's really seen Kuwait or Iraq.

"It's different traveling with the Marine Corps because you don't get to see anything," he says. "You just see it through the back of a truck."

He joined the Marine reserves on a spur-of-the-moment decision. "I didn't know what I wanted, and I figured I might as well join the Marines," Alvarado says.

He misses his spare time. "Here, the only time off you have is at night. I'd like some time during the day to read a magazine and not read it under a red lens."

He misses his dog, a fat Dalmatian named Cupid. "She used to have a heart on her nose but grew more spots, so now people can't see the heart," he says, smiling. "They think it's stupid that her name is Cupid now."

He misses hearing the complaints of his roommate, Joe Gropp. They share a house in Peoria.

"I miss him bitching at me for putting ashes in a dish, instead of in the ashtray," Alvarado says. "I do the dishes, but he finds it disgusting. He doesn't smoke, and he'll follow me around the house turning on fans and opening windows. ... But he's a pretty boy and brings girls back to the house."

He misses eating meals, usually once a week, with his mother.

"She's always traveling, so she doesn't have normal meals," he says. "She'll throw a bunch of leftovers together, some of it from her travels, and make a crazy casserole."

But for everything his misses, Alvarado knows there is another side to the equation.

When he was in boot camp, he missed many of the same things, but when he got home, he realized he hadn't really missed them after all.

"You'd do something again or eat something and say, 'Ah, this isn't that cool,' " he says. "You don't really miss it."

He already knows what he'll miss about Iraq.

He'll miss sitting on post, late at night, looking at the sky on a cloudless night.

"They have some of the best stars here," he says. "The sky is so bright. There are no trees, so you see the whole sky."

He's going to miss reveille. Every morning at 6:30, somebody walks by the tents, screaming "Reveille, reveille!" Back in Peoria, Alvarado had a hard time waking up. He'd hit the snooze button or not touch the alarm at all. Then, his roommate would come in and yell at him to turn it off. He likes the Marine routine.

And he's going to miss the people, he says.

"I'm so close to these people. It's like having 13 best friends."

April 13, 2003

NAME: Sgt. Brian Dollinger
RANK: Marine sergeant
AGE: 30
HOMETOWN: Morton, Ill.
DUTY: Combat engineer, Charlie Company,
6th Engineer Support Battalion

Beethoven symphony would sound great

CAMP CHESTY, central Iraq — All of the Marines have their different dates: the day they hope to be home and the day they think they'll be home.

Sgt. Brian Dollinger hopes to be home by May 30, when his daughter Arianna turns 3.

"I'm hoping to get back by then," he says. "And I know I'll be home in time for my wife's birthday in July. Every day that goes by, I get a little more concerned that I won't make it. That time line is starting to crunch down."

Dollinger, 30, is a combat engineer with 6th Engineer Support Battalion. It is the middle of April, and he is hoping to get back by October at the latest. His commanders are not as optimistic.

"Even though the mission is complete, there are different things we can do as engineers," Dollinger says. "I'm ready for it to be done. But I know how long it took us to come over — all the stages it took to get to California and then to get over here. I'm apprehensive about how long it will take to get back."

Dollinger, a Marine reservist, is a doctoral student in music at Ball State University. His specialties are conducting orchestras and playing the bass.

He was one semester from finishing his course work when he was deployed. He doesn't know when he'll get a chance to finish. "Certain classes are offered only at certain times and not every year," Dollinger says. "That may be a problem when I get back."

After he earns his doctorate, he hopes to teach at the university level.

"Hopefully, it's a position like Ball State where I'll conduct the orchestras, I'll teach conducting, teach bass and then have a professional local symphony as well," he says.

His wife, Sabina, is also a doctoral music student at Ball State. They were married before he had to report.

"It's been a learning experience to watch people adapt and cope with issues," he says. "Not everybody adapts very well. The ones you wouldn't think would be very strong have really come forward. I've been very surprised by a lot of Marines, how strong they've been and how they were able to pull through."

Dollinger has spent most of his time in Iraq fortifying positions and doing security detail. His main concern is losing a finger.

"When I'm doing barbed wire, yes, I think about it," he says. "If I lost a finger on my left hand, that would hurt me big time. ... As far as conducting, if I lost my right arm, I could conduct with my left.

"When I'm doing the explosives, I'm not thinking about losing a finger. If something goes wrong, I'll lose more than a finger."

He plays with five professional orchestras.

"Everybody needs a bass player," he says.

When he gets back from the war, Dollinger plans to dedicate a performance to Marines who died. "There are tons of pieces out there that are used in memorial concerts," he says. "I'm going to have a moment of silence and play a piece for them."

While Dollinger is starving to hear some classical music, he has seen a benefit to being around so many young Marines with a variety of musical tastes.

"I would give anything for a Beethoven symphony right now — a quartet, anything," he says. "But I've been hearing all kinds of music from the younger Marines. I can't even pronounce some of the names of these groups, can't understand some of the things they are saying, but it's different music and interesting to hear it. Once in a while, I'll even get a good country tune."

April 12, 2003

CHAPTER 7

Casualties: 'It hurts me when I see people hurting.'

April 6, 2003

NAME: Sarah Weddle
RANK: Army private 1st class
AGE: 19
HOMETOWN: Independence, Mo.
DUTY: Combat medic, 546th Medical Company,
Ft. Hood, Texas

Young medic will forever see the faces of those she's treated

EAST OF NASIRIYAH, Iraq — Pfc. Sarah Weddle sits in the sunshine with tired eyes.

"It hurts me when I see people hurting," she says, clasping her hands tightly.

At night, when she tries to sleep on a green cot under a scratchy green blanket, not far from the tent where she works as a medic, she remembers their faces.

The adorable little girl who lost her mother in a gunfight.

"We think the mother pushed the girl under the dash in her car," Weddle says. "She was fine. She was so cute, but it was so sad."

The man whose arms were peppered with gunshot wounds. He was holding two children in his lap, trying to cradle and comfort them, when they were struck with bullets.

The man who didn't look like a man; his entire body was covered with burns. His kidneys shut down, and his organs failed, and he slipped away on her watch. He died right there in front of her.

"It was so scary," she says. "He looked so bad. I mean, he had no skin left. I've never even seen a dead person before. I've never seen anything like that. I just got out of high school."

She tries to sleep, but she sees their faces and remembers their stories and hears their voices, even the voices of Iraqis, the enemy prisoners of war (EPWs). She can't understand their broken English, and she wishes she was back home in Independence, Mo., back where it's safe and warm, with her family.

She never thought she'd miss her family, but she does.

Back in her bedroom with a closet filled with clothes, mostly pinks and baby blue.

"I love clothes, colorful clothes, but now I only wear beige," she says.

Back when she felt normal, back when she could do her long blond hair and paint her nails, she was an admitted girlie girl, who shocked them all when she joined the Army.

She's not that person anymore.

No longer a child. Not yet a crass old veteran.

She's somewhere in between.

She begins to cry, lying in her cot, unable to sleep.

"I've been crying a lot lately," she says. "It's so hard. I think, 'Why do I have to be doing this?' I think, 'Why am I out here?' I don't understand it sometimes."

And then, she thinks of her patients.

She tries to comfort them. The Americans and Iraqis. Doesn't matter. She tries to be cheerful and upbeat, but it's all an act.

And it's getting harder every day.

The veteran medics joke about death.

But she can't joke.

She's too young, too fresh.

She's been out of high school for only nine months. She just got out of boot camp. And now she's in the middle of a war.

"I had a scholarship to a community college, and I didn't really want to do that," she says. "Everybody was shocked when I joined. I wanted to do something different with my life. I didn't think I was ready to go to college yet. To me, that seems too easy. Everybody goes to college after high school. I wanted to do something different. I wanted to see some things; I was afraid if I didn't do it now, I would never do it."

She questions the decision every day.

"I think, 'Why did I do this?'" she says. "My parents write me and say, 'If I would have known you were going to be there right now, I wouldn't have let you join.'"

Weddle works for an area support medical com-

April 6, 2003

pany, which has moved six or seven times since the start of the war.

"We move a lot," she says. "We haven't been anywhere for longer than two weeks. We are supposed to be able to put up and take down real quick."

Her unit was supposed to move farther north, stopping outside Baghdad to take care of EPWs, but a convoy got ambushed along the same route they were going to take, and the plans were scuttled.

"They told us we wouldn't be pushing forward," she says. "I was so grateful because I was so scared. I want to wait for things to settle down; I don't want to go forward at all. There are a lot of people who say, 'I want to go forward.' But I'm sorry, I'm so new at everything; it scares me; I'm not going to lie."

She called home a few days ago and talked to her parents. That helped a little.

Her squad leader told her to take some time off, to go watch a few movies, and that helped, too.

She watched "Minority Report" starring Tom Cruise, which she found strange. But for a few hours, she felt normal again – like she was back home.

"Anything that reminds me of home is wonderful," she says. "The last couple of days have been really hard. It's very stressful. I don't get a lot of rest, so it's real hard. But I read my Bible a lot."

She decided to paint her nails. Bright pink.

"I know we aren't supposed to paint our nails, but I did anyway," she says. "I have a habit of biting my nails if they aren't painted. I said, 'OK, we are at war, I'm painting my nails.' I don't care. It's the only girlie girl thing I have, the only thing I can do."

No longer a child. Not yet a crass old veteran.

She doesn't jump anymore when she hears an explosion — it's happened so often she can't remember anymore — and isn't that strange, how she doesn't even flinch? It doesn't bother her anymore to go a couple days without a shower. Or to push meds through an intravenous line. Or to work with the EPWs.

"I'm thinking about re-upping," she says. "I'm thinking of doing 20 years and then retiring."

April 12, 2003

NAME: Sarah Cade
RANK: Navy petty officer 3rd class
AGE: 27
HOMETOWN: Detroit, Mich.
DUTY: Corpsman, 2nd Medical Battalion

For corpsman, it's hard to help the enemy

CAMP CHESTY, central Iraq — No. 220 sits under a camouflage net, at the Navy surgical hospital, looking absolutely harmless.

She wears a pink-and-orange dress and has a braid of long black hair down her back. She has a shrapnel wound on her side.

Navy Petty Officer 3rd Class Sarah Cade, a Navy corpsman from Detroit, treats the injury, which is not life-threatening.

No. 221 sits on the same cot.

The woman, in her mid-30s, is wrapped in a silver blanket. She wears a purple-and-gold dress, and her head is covered with a scarf.

Cade bandages her right foot. The woman starts to cry, holding her hands in her face, wiping away tears.

"Your family is in the back," Cade says. "They are all right."

The women say they are Iraqi civilians. Cade treats them with respect, giving them warmth and compassion, even though she doesn't trust them.

"They came in, and they said their car was all shot up," Cade says. "They came in with two males, and the women said the males are their brothers. But you don't know if the males are civilian or military, and the women could be in on it, too."

No matter who comes to this Navy surgical hospital — Marines, Iraqi civilians or enemy prisoners of war — they are treated the same. As soon as the injured arrive, usually by helicopter, each patient is tracked by a number written on the back of his or her hand.

"The thing that's really hard for corpsmen is we are here to take care of our Marines," Cade says. "But we have to take care of somebody who is trying to hurt us. And that's very, very hard for me to see. I don't want to see the EPWs. I don't want to give them any water, but it's my job, and I do it. And I take pride in taking care of them."

April 12, 2003

She says it comes by instinct: "It's a mother thing. If you see a baby fall and scrape their knee, your instinct is to pick that child back up."

As she treats the patients, she is protected by a Marine security detail, armed with M16 rifles.

"My Marines take care of me," Cade says. "They don't leave my side."

Cade, 27, was born and raised in Detroit, in a family with five brothers and sisters. She graduated from Mackenzie High School. While attending Wayne County Community College, she had a daughter, Marcia Black, 7. Cade tried to work, go to school and raise a child as a single parent, but it was too hard.

"It didn't seem like I had enough time to be with her," Cade says.

Six years ago, she joined the Navy.

"It's fun," she says. "It's a good experience. I'm glad I joined. I'm going to reenlist for three years and then get out."

While Cade is deployed in Iraq, her daughter is in Detroit with her grandmother, Valencia Grier.

It's only the second time Cade has been away from her daughter.

The hard part was pulling her out of school in Jacksonville, N.C.

"I was so upset, I cried," Cade says. "I took her out in December, right after Christmas, and enrolled her in a school in Detroit. She already had a best friend and sleepovers. That hurt me. It really did. I'd like for her to be with me, but Grandma is the next best thing."

Cade is stationed out of Camp Lejeune, N.C., and works with the 2nd Medical Battalion.

This is her first time in a combat zone, and she has seen several gruesome injuries.

April 12, 2003

"Some dude got shot three times in the head," Cade says. "One came out his eye. He was also shot in the back."

She feels a sense of gratification treating Marines.

"They are very grateful that you even sit and talk to them. I ask them: How you doing? Where are you from? Everything is going to be OK."

Her unit has moved several times, moving north through Iraq, from Breach Point West, to Camp Viper, to Camp Anderson, to Camp Chesty. Soon, she expects it to move even closer to Baghdad.

"I don't think this war is over," she says. "I say I should be home by June 15. That's my guesstimation right now. That's my prediction.

"I'm ready to go home. I've been here too long. But we can't go home until the war is over, and I'm fine with that."

April 12, 2003

April 4, 2003

NAME: Russell Green
RANK: Navy petty officer 1st class
AGE: 37
HOMETOWN: Ritter, S.C.
DUTY: Guarding enemy prisoners
of war at Fleet Hospital No. 3

He feels sorry for prisoners but stays alert

CAMP VIPER, southern Iraq — Petty Officer 1st Class Russell Green sits at the door in an aluminum chair, armed with a 9mm pistol, keeping an eye on a group of Iraqi soldiers who are prisoners of war.

The Iraqis wear blue hospital gowns and plastic handcuffs. They sleep in beds in an air-conditioned tent, filling up an entire ward at Fleet Hospital No. 3.

"One guy must have stepped on a land mine," Green says. "His foot was split to where you could see the bone. I'm not a corpsman, and I haven't worked on this side of the military, and it's an eye-opener. It's like wow. I kind of feel sorry for them. You are talking about a human life here, good or bad. I've never seen some injuries like that before."

Green, 37, of Ritter, S.C., works a 12-hour shift at the Navy hospital every day.

"My job is normally going out to sea," Green says. "Coming into the desert is nothing I've ever had to do before. I usually ride ships."

Most of the Iraqis are quiet. Security personnel don't let Iraqis speak Arabic for fear they could plan an attack on a doctor or nurse.

"Today was the first day they have all been awake at all times," Green says. "We haven't had any problems. No agitation. No nothing. Nothing. This group we have, I hope they are all like this.

"As far as food and medical care, it's probably better than they've ever gotten. It's not the best food in the world, but it's probably better than they are used to. They are definitely getting first-class medical attention."

When an ambulance arrives at the hospital, someone from security has to search the Iraqis and put handcuffs on them before a doctor or nurse can treat them.

"Some come in wearing military outfits," Green says. "Nine times out of 10, their clothes have already been removed. A couple came in blue or brown uniforms."

Most of the time, an investigator talks immediately to the prisoner to try to determine whether he is a civilian or a soldier.

"If you got a guy who is well-fed, hair cut, nice trimmed mustache, you know he's Republican Guard," Green says. "You know he's somewhere up there."

Regular Iraqi soldiers wear ragged clothes. They are usually skinny and famished. "One guy said, 'If I didn't join, they would kill my family,'" Green says.

The hospital was built in less than a week. Most of the first patients were prisoners.

"At first, we watched every little thing because we didn't know what to expect. Now, it's interesting. Every day, I see how they are getting better. People who weren't sitting up are now sitting up. One guy was washing his face. Another guy was combing his hair."

Green stands 5 feet 9 and weighs 180 pounds, about 20 less than when he arrived in Iraq.

"All the diets I tried back home weren't working," he says with a smile. "So I decided, I'll try the desert diet."

After 19 years in the Navy, Green plans to retire next year. He and his wife, Karen, have been married for 17 years and have two children.

"Most of the time, I'm a ship serviceman who runs the ship store, barbershop and laundry," Green says. "When I retire, I'll probably go into retail sales."

April 12, 2003

NAME: John Furr
RANK: Navy petty officer 3rd class
AGE: 26
HOMETOWN: Belmont, N.C.
DUTY: Ambulance driver at Bravo
Company surgical hospital

Ambulance driver hears birds in his sleep

CAMP CHESTY, central Iraq — Petty Officer 3rd Class John Furr sleeps on top of his ambulance and listens for the birds.

Helicopters.

"I hear birds in my sleep," he says. "When I wake up, I think I hear a helicopter, but it's just a truck going by. Most of the time, we sleep on top of the ambulances. We can tell what's coming in, if they are circling around us."

As soon as a helicopter touches down and the dust clears, an ambulance is on the scene to rush patients to the Bravo Company surgical hospital.

There are only four ambulance drivers, and they work round the clock. Furr of Belmont, N.C., drives an ambulance he's named the Red-Headed Sand Machine because of the color of his hair.

"I haven't seen the front lines, but I see the patients coming in off the front lines," he says. "I don't know what those guys are going through. ... I have tremendous respect for these guys — to get shot and wounded and take shrapnel. They are putting themselves on the line for our country. These guys are young guys."

Furr holds their hands and tries to calm them down, to give them some comfort.

He has transported three U.S. soldiers who were killed in action. "You know they have families and kids," he says. "I think about their families more than them.

"We have a chaplain and a religious petty officer. They say the last words for the body. Then, we have a morgue team that tries to get them out of here in 24 hours. It's a quick turnaround. They prep the body. That's the most important thing, getting the body back home. The KIAs are burned into your memory. When you go to sleep, that's what you see."

Furr carries a Bible and a hymnal in his pocket. "If they are Christians and they are scared, I'll hand them a Bible, or they'll ask me to read it to them," he says. "Being a Christian, it makes me feel good."

Furr wasn't a Christian until he married his wife, Angela.

"Her family is really religious, and I fought it for a while — but it got me," he says. "I'm glad to be a born-again Christian. I pray every day, morning, night. That's exactly what's getting me through it. I get letters from my wife and know that our church is praying for us. That makes me feel good and it keeps me going."

Furr, who has been on active duty for eight years, is based at Camp Lejeune, N.C., as a dental technician.

"I joined in high school, my senior year," he says. "My hometown is a textile town, and I didn't want to go into that. ... I wanted to be an electronics technician. I went to the recruiter, and all the jobs were filled. And then I became a dental tech, so I could get a trade out of it."

This is his second deployment overseas. His first was in Bosnia. "It was right after the war," he says. "I saw a lot of kids, a lot of land-mine injuries."

In Iraq, while helping a prisoner of war out of an ambulance, he was sprayed and covered with blood.

He was shook up but kept working, taking patients to the hospital before getting cleaned up.

"That was my main concern: take care of the patients and get them to the hospital," he says.

Furr has been married four years. "We are trying to have kids. We put it off until after the deployment."

He was going to get out 1½ years ago, but the couple want kids and decided to have the military pay for it. "I reenlisted, and we came over. I don't regret it. If you drive through Iraq and see the kids, they are starving. They've been repressed so long. I honestly believe the people here want us here. The Iraqis are not taking care of their own."

As the war winds down, he is getting more anxious to leave. "If they told me I could leave tonight, it would take me 5 minutes to pack my bags," he says. "There's no doubt I'm going to make it home. I'm going to be back as soon as I can."

April 12, 2003

NAME: Matt Orme
RANK: Navy lieutenant commander
AGE: 33
HOMETOWN: St. Joseph, Mich.
DUTY: Emergency-room physician in charge
of the triage area for a mobile surgical hospital in Iraq

A front-row seat in the classroom of war

CAMP CHESTY, central Iraq — Lt. Cmdr. Matt Orme lets out a smile.

"We just showered for the first time in 10 days," he says. "It was a big deal. It was awesome. If I have three layers of grit, I probably got two of them off."

He has learned to enjoy the simple pleasures because his job is so horrific.

Orme is an emergency-room physician in charge of the Shock, Stabilization and Triage Area for a Navy surgical hospital in Iraq.

"It's like a mini-emergency department," he says.

Orme runs a staff with four doctors, four nurses and 16 corpsmen.

"The hardest stuff is working on the Iraqi kids, those who are caught in the cross fire or used as a human shield," Orme says. "We've seen some pretty horrific injuries to small children."

Orme has a 20-month-old child, Ali, about the same age as the children he has treated.

"Last night, we had a child with a penetrating wound to the skull, with a brain injury," he says. "Last week, we were down at Camp Anderson, and there was a child whose face, nose and mouth had pretty much been blown off. It was pretty shaking to everybody involved.

"That evening, we had the combat stress people — the psychologists and psychiatrists — come and talk to people and tell them that it's OK to talk about it among yourselves. It's OK to be upset by that.

"Since we are the first ones to see things, we usually see the goriest stuff. We have a good relationship with our combat stress folks."

Orme joined the Navy on its medical school scholarship program, graduating from Indiana University's medical school.

"The Navy paid for med school, and I've been in for eight years," he says. "I'll be out in about another year. This is my last stop with the Navy. I got selected, invited — whatever you call it — to come out here."

Orme will finish his commitment in about 16 months. He plans to become an ER doctor.

"This is an experience that almost no physician gets to do: come out here and actually see combat injuries," Orme says. "If you see combat injuries, there are few things that will rattle you or make you nervous. From that standpoint, it's a great experience."

He usually works as an ER doctor at the naval hospital at Camp Lejeune, N.C. The pace and the type of injuries are significantly different in Iraq.

"You might see a gunshot wound every couple of months back home," he says.

Orme treats Americans and Iraqis, but he has noticed a big difference between the types of injuries.

The Americans have suffered a lot of extremity wounds.

"Their body armor is so good — the flak jacket and Kevlar helmets," he says. "The Iraqi civilians and military don't have the same protection."

The Iraqis have suffered more serious wounds.

"I'd say the majority of serious thorax wounds are from the Iraqis," Orme says.

The one thing that has surprised him is the human body.

"First of all, the human body can take a lot of gunshots without dying," Orme says. "At home, you see one guy, who got shot one or two times, and they come in dead. Here, you are constantly amazed at the resilience of the human body. Here, you see somebody who was next to a grenade that went off and they may have some bad injuries, but they are able to survive it. That's been a big surprise."

Orme sleeps in a tent on a cot, about 18 inches from the next cot. He goes for runs to get rid of stress. But the one thing that makes him happy is when he gets letters from his wife, Kate.

He closes every letter to his wife by writing: "We are doing a good job. I miss you guys. And hopefully, I'll be home soon."

April 12, 2003

NAME: DeAngelo Stroman
RANK: Marine lance corporal
AGE: 19
HOMETOWN: Pontiac, Mich.
DUTY: Security at a Navy surgical hospital

Medicine amazes Michigan Marine

CAMP CHESTY, central Iraq — The enemy prisoner of war sits naked in the sand, covered with a shiny silver blanket, his hands tied with plastic bands.

Lance Cpl. DeAngelo Stroman stands about 4 feet away, holding an M16 rifle.

The man refuses to talk, refuses to cooperate, and Stroman has to wait for a translator before the man is taken into the surgical hospital, about 80 miles south of Baghdad. The prisoner doesn't appear to have any serious injuries.

"My shock trauma platoon, which is like a mobile surgical company, has seen 100 patients, and I'd say almost 75 percent or more has been EPWs," he says, referring to enemy prisoners of war. "Most of them stay quiet. ... You just want to watch them."

Stroman of Pontiac, Mich., is not afraid. He stands 5 feet 10 and weighs 210 pounds. Most of the prisoners are small in stature and look weak.

"There are a lot of people around," Stroman says. "The EPWs are unarmed, so they can't really do anything to you. Me? I'm a pretty big guy."

Stroman was raised in a family with four sisters and two brothers. He played football, basketball and baseball at Pontiac Northern High School.

"I was pretty good at football," he says. "I played a lot of sports to stay out of trouble."

Stroman's wife, Shaneka Stroman, talked him into joining the Marines 1½ years ago.

"It was my wife's decision," he says. "I wasn't really doing anything but getting in trouble. She sat me down and had a nice little conversation, and then I saw a recruiter. From there — boom! — that's how it happened."

Stroman is trained to be a motor transport driver, called a Motor T. But he's been on security detail in Iraq.

"My recruiter said, 'Go Motor T because it's really fun. You won't be away from your family a lot.'

"I said, 'All right. Good to go. I'll go Motor T.' Before I knew it, I was here."

He's been in Kuwait or Iraq for more than two months, watching the doctors make medical magic.

"Watching the doctors work is amazing," Stroman says. "We had one guy, an Iraqi, come in with three shots to his head, and our team was working hard, and they brought him back. I was watching. I was curious. It's eye-opening. It makes you appreciate a lot of stuff, more than you usually would."

When he gets out of the Marines in about three years, he plans to go to college.

"I haven't decided yet," Stroman says. "Hopefully, I'll have it better planned when I get back. But I want to go to school and get an associate's degree in business management or something, so I can get out and explore on my own."

Stroman and his wife have a daughter, Taylor.

"I miss home a lot," he says. "I miss everything. Snow. Real food. Ice water."

MIKE NACE

April 12, 2003

NAME: Mike Nace (opposite page; patients' names unknown)
RANK: Navy lieutenant commander
AGE: 42
HOMETOWN: Hemet, Calif.
DUTY: En route care nurse, Fleet Hospital

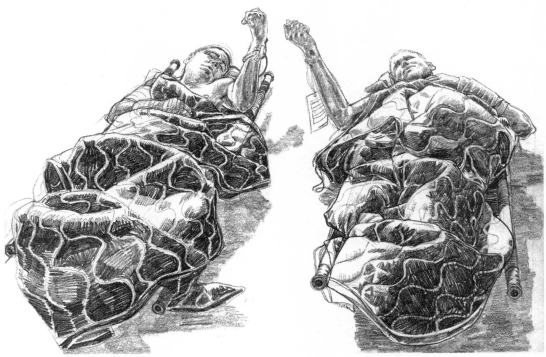

April 12, 2003

Medics work quickly with heavy traumas

CAMP CHESTY, central Iraq — Lt. Cmdr. Mike Nace gets off the helicopter and faces the ambulance, holding up four fingers.

"Four injured?" the ambulance driver asks.

No, Nace gestures. "We need four ambulances."

Three of the injured walk down the helicopter ramp with their arms in slings. One man is limping so badly that another Marine has to help him to the ambulance.

Nace disappears into the helicopter and comes off with a Marine on a stretcher. The Marine is rushed to the Navy surgical hospital in the back of an ambulance.

At the same time, another helicopter unloads a string of enemy prisoners of war.

Thirteen patients show up at once. The hospital staff is used to it.

The medics and doctors work quickly, trying to figure out who should be treated first.

Two Marines lie side by side on stretchers. They punch hands, giving each other encouragement.

Nace stays with a Marine who was injured about 18 hours earlier in a suicide bombing in Baghdad. While the major battles of this war appear over, Nace says he believes the real danger now will come from terrorist attacks.

"We had four or five Marines and eight to 10 civilians who had shrapnel injuries from a terrorist," Nace says. "They were getting ready to set up a defensive perimeter. A bunch of people were hollering and waving, happy to see the guys. Somebody broke through, and they said he had a bomb on his back, detonated it and took all these people out with the Marines."

Nace has been up all night, working on the injured at a trauma unit about 7 miles from Baghdad. It's about a 40-minute flight to this surgical hospital.

"Last night, because things were frantic, we actually filled the four beds we have for resuscitation, and we had two more waiting to come in," Nace says. "We have two operating rooms, and we worked both."

A 4-year-old girl was injured in the bombing. She had a skull fracture and a stomach injury. Part of her arm was gone, and she was missing a finger.

"We are using stuff that isn't made for kids," Nace says. "We are supposed to be using it on adults. We are improvising and adapting for pediatrics."

Nace transfers the Marine to a doctor, while giving a quick summary: "He has shrapnel to the leg, shrapnel to the arm. We opened him up and found puncture wounds in his belly. We had to take out a piece of his belly. Had to take out a piece of his intestines. They packed him, but didn't close it,

though. He had significant blood loss. We've been watching his vital signs and keeping him."

Nace has been in the Navy almost 24 years and has worked his way up.

"They sent me back to do my undergrad and sent me back to do my master's in trauma critical care with an emphasis in emergency medicine," he says.

He is about to transfer to Quantico, Va., where he will be a student for 10 months. Then, he'll go to a command.

This is his fifth time on deployment to another country. He did Operation Desert Storm and Desert Shield against Iraq, as well as Bosnia and Beirut.

"We are moving faster as far as the medical part," he says. "Last time, during Desert Storm, we set up right behind the breach. We were about 6 miles back. We saw 750 patients in five days, and we were a big group. In the last five days, we've seen 132 patients. Yesterday, we had 13" operating room cases.

And that's at a small trauma unit.

"We've seen a lot of kids," he says. "We didn't think we would see a lot of kids."

Nace has three children of his own. As much as he wants to see his family, he thinks he'll be in Iraq for a while.

"I don't think this war is even close to being done," he says.

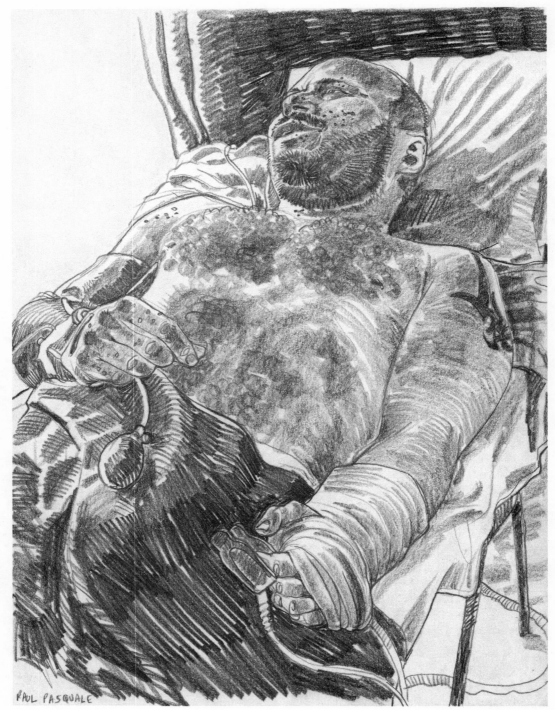

PAUL PASQUALE

April 12, 2003

NAME: Paul Pasquale (opposite)
AGE: 36
HOMETOWN: London, England
DUTY: Cameraman for Reuters news service

NAME: Samia Nakhoul (below)
AGE: 42
HOMETOWN: Beirut, Lebanon
DUTY: Writer for Reuters news service

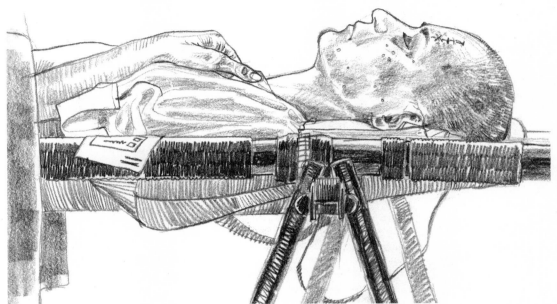

April 12, 2003

War journalists embrace dangerous job

CAMP CHESTY, central Iraq — Paul Pasquale lies on a gurney in a Navy surgical hospital, covered with wounds and bandages, looking like he was attacked by sharks.

Pasquale, 36, of London is a cameraman for Reuters news service. He was on the 15th floor of the Palestine Hotel in Baghdad when he was injured one week ago by a tank shell.

He has wounds on his cheeks, nose, around his lips, hands, arms, down his side, across his chest, over his hip and down to his feet.

He lifts up the sheets to show the wounds on his legs. Some look like little punctures. Others snake across his side in a bizarre pattern, as if a child had scribbled over his body with a Magic Marker.

"But I've still got my testicles," he says.

Samia Nakhoul, 42, a writer for Reuters, was injured with Pasquale. Two other journalists were killed in the attack.

They were part of a different kind of war coverage — more upclose than ever before, the military promised. It included the new approach of having journalists embedded, or assigned to specific military units. Journalists would be at the front lines. They would see the fighting.

Ten journalists have died during the Iraq war — some in accidents, some from bombs and bullets. No incident has drawn more attention than the Palestine Hotel shelling.

Nakhoul and Pasquale don't assign blame or express regret.

"I've been doing it for 13 years," Nakhoul says. "I

like to chase the story. I don't regret it. This is part of the deal."

Wars are kind of a specialty, Pasquale says. "I haven't missed a war in 15 years — Bosnia, Rwanda, Kosovo, Afghanistan. You name it, really."

But Iraq, he says, is different.

"I changed my job on this one," he says. "Most of my job is as a cameraman, so you have to be at the front to get the film. This is the first war where I've waited for the war to come to me. ... It was extraordinary. It was like waiting for a tidal wave at a beach, holding on."

Before the shelling, Nakhoul was on the hotel balcony, watching the fighting.

"I had the phone; I was filing to our main desk, telling them what I was seeing."

The writer, who covered the 1991 Persian Gulf War, has been in Baghdad for about six weeks. Her eyelids are streaked red and purple, set against a pale yellow background.

She is peppered with cuts on her cheek, forehead, nose and chin.

A piece of shrapnel sliced into her forehead and settled in her head. "I had brain surgery four days ago to clean it up," she says.

She doesn't know the extent of the damage. "They'll have to do tests," she says.

She opens her mouth and a nurse takes her temperature, as another inserts an IV stem.

"Don't bend your arm," he says.

She squeezes her eyes in pain.

At the same time, doctors work on Pasquale.

He tried to carry a friend out of the rubble, but his hands were injured. "I just crawled out," he says. "I wasn't feeling too great, put it that way. I didn't feel I was dead, but I felt like I was on the way out."

He has been in Baghdad for six months. He had the option to leave, but he wanted to stay. "I was running part of the operation, and I employed a lot of Iraqis — a lot of fixers, a lot of people like that. For me to ... leave the work to the Iraqis, I just couldn't do that."

As he is taken to the ward, he is asked whether he will cover the next war.

"I don't know," he says. "Ask me in a year."

April 5, 2003

NAME: Jody Stenquist
RANK: Navy petty officer 1st class
AGE: 29
HOMETOWN: Pontiac, Mich.
DUTY: Corpsman, Fleet Hospital No. 3

There's a certain magic in the desert

CAMP VIPER, southern Iraq — Petty Officer 1st Class Jody Stenquist has seen the magic.

"The docs are making magic here," she says about Fleet Hospital No. 3 in southern Iraq.

Stenquist, 29, of Pontiac, Mich., is a corpsman, working on a casualty receiving team.

"It's amazing what they are doing with the limited supplies we have. We aren't getting one or two patients at a time. We are getting five, six or seven at a time."

This is the first time a fleet hospital has been set up in Iraq. They are still working through some of the bugs. "We don't have the normal things you would have," Stenquist says. "We don't have Band-Aids. We are using gauze and things like that. I guess they didn't come. We still have containers with gear in it that haven't been opened yet. Some of our equipment is 20 years old, and they packed it up in the ISO containers. We didn't know how to work the suction machines. We are cutting tubing off other things to connect to suction machines."

Despite the obstacles of setting up a hospital in the desert, they have made it work. Last week, two ambulances rolled up, unannounced, with seven patients.

The U.S. service members were injured in a motor vehicle accident. Some of the injuries included broken femurs, a broken back and head trauma. Stenquist started to ask some questions: "Where were you? How has it gone? Are there a lot of injuries?"

This is the first time Stenquist has been in a combat zone and she's been frustrated because she doesn't have any sense of the big picture. She doesn't know what's going on.

"We get very little intel here," she says. "It was great to be able to talk to these guys, to let them know we are working our butts off here, too."

Stenquist pulls eight-hour shifts every day.

When an ambulance arrives at the hospital, she meets the rig outside. Security personnel check the Iraqi patients, and Stenquist does a quick triage.

"We can't bring anybody in until they are checked by security," Stenquist says. "Security checks them before we even touch them. None of our people are allowed weapons.

"The trick is keeping a clear mind. We are getting all varieties of nationalities. We don't treat the patients; we treat the injuries. We will treat anyone who is injured."

They have seen everything from multiple gunshot wounds to motor vehicle accidents. "A lot of the junior corpsmen are amazed at the types of injuries we are getting with the limited amount of equipment we have," she says. "We're just making things up. We are making magic."

Stenquist grew up in Pontiac and her family lives in Auburn Hills, Mich. She attended Eastern Michigan University for nursing.

"I was only 17 when I went, and I wasn't sure if that's what I wanted to do," she says. "I figured joining the military and getting 12 weeks of school to be a corpsman and having that medical experience would let me know if that's what I wanted to do. I've just enjoyed it and stayed."

She has been on active duty for almost 10 years and plans to do another 10 and retire.

"We can do everything, like a physician assistant," she says. "We are doing sutures, procedures, putting in chest tubes, intubating patients, pushing morphine."

For Stenquist, the only real negative part has been being away from her daughter, Victoria Tison, who turned 1 on April 10. Victoria is staying with her father, Blake Tison, in Pensacola, Fla.

"It was really hard," Stenquist says. "I spent the last seven years with the Marines, and I came to shore duty to have a baby and finish school. It was harder than I thought it was going to be to leave her. I think it's harder on me than her."

April 7, 2003

NAME: Tim Power
RANK: Marine corporal
AGE: 25
HOMETOWN: Bloomington, Ill.
DUTY: Supply/Headquarters, Charlie Company,
6th Engineer Support Battalion

Humvee crash puts Marine on new path

EAST OF NASIRIYAH, Iraq — Driving a Humvee down a highway through the Iraqi desert, Cpl. Tim Power takes off his helmet and wipes sweat from his forehead. A big thick cloud of dust blinds him for a split second.

He doesn't see the other Humvees in the convoy slam on their brakes. Doesn't have time to react until it's too late. He hears the bang as he plows into the backend of another Humvee, going about 45 m.p.h. He sees a bright white flash, as his jaw hits the steering wheel.

Maj. Michael McCarthy, who is sitting in the passenger seat, flies forward, his head striking the dashboard.

Power sees him go limp and fall out the door.

The Humvee is heading into a ditch, right where Power thinks McCarthy has landed. He wrenches the steering wheel to the left, hoping the Humvee doesn't run over McCarthy.

It comes to a stop and Power stumbles out.

"I killed the major," he thinks as he walks over to him.

"I'm so sorry," Power says, over and over.

McCarthy has a nasty cut above his forehead, down to the bone.

"I can see his brain," Power thinks.

McCarthy is groggy, incoherent for about 5 minutes.

Power's face is covered with blood.

"The major wasn't in good shape at all," Power says. "The first couple of minutes, he was pretty disoriented. I think we were all kind of shocked. It took him about 5 minutes to come to and realize what happened and where he was."

Thirteen Marines were injured in the chain-reaction accident, although most suffered only cuts and bruises. McCarthy and two other Marines are sent to an Army Area Support Medical Company, east of Nasiriyah.

Cpl. Tim Powers writes letters home inside a Humvee during a sandstorm.

March 26, 2003

McCarthy, in charge of Charlie Company, 6th Engineer Support Battalion, gets stitches on his forehead.

Power has his jaw X-rayed, and the results are inconclusive.

Gunnery Sgt. Michael Stein, 37, of East Peoria, Ill., has bruised ribs on his left side. He was sitting in the back of a Humvee, across from Master Sgt. Garland Powell, 40, of Sardis, Ohio. Powell has bruised ribs.

After a few hours, McCarthy is feeling better. He's outside, walking around and acting silly. Doctors had to cut off his biochem suit, which is worn to counteract biological or chemical attack, and he walks around in pants that are cut off at the knees.

"I got the Gilligan look," McCarthy says.

The first batch of X rays suggest that Power has a broken jaw. He has two or three stitches in the corner of his mouth.

They spend the night on cots in a big green tent. And they get a big treat: cold chocolate milk. Nobody can remember the last time they had something cold. In the desert, a glass of water comes warm or hot.

In the morning, Power tries to eat Froot Loops, using one side of his mouth.

Dr. Mike Curtis, a Navy captain, walks up to him outside.

"I don't want them to wire my mouth up," Power says.

"Yeah, but you want your mouth to work in the future," Curtis says.

"I don't know if I'll be able to eat an MRE," Power says, referring to meals ready to eat.

"We'll get you a lot of that raspberry ground stuff," Curtis says, laughing.

Power, 25, of Bloomington, Ill., works in Supply/ Headquarters for Charlie Company, 6th Engineer Support Battalion.

"I help the company gunny with the beans, bullets and bandages," Power says.

Another doctor reads the X rays, but they are still inconclusive.

Power is sent back to Camp Viper with the other Marines.

The next day, he is sent to Kuwait City, where he gets more treatment.

It is unclear whether he will return to Charlie Company or whether he will be sent home.

"If I got to go home, it would be bittersweet," he says. "I'd be upset that I came over here and didn't finish it out. Then again, once I went home and saw my wife and family, I'd probably forget all about it."

April 12, 2003

NAME: Joey Coleman
RANK: Marine lance corporal
AGE: 20
HOMETOWN: Dover, Del.
DUTY: Heavy-equipment operator,
3rd Assault Amphibious Battalion

Artist fears an injury to his right hand

CAMP CHESTY, central Iraq — Lance Cpl. Joey Coleman waits outside a Navy surgical hospital. His right hand hangs limp and swollen.

"My right hand is my life," says Coleman, who is right-handed. "It's my biggest fear: if anything happens to my right hand. I just don't want any scar tissue."

Coleman, 20, a Marine reservist, is studying to become a cartoonist. He had smashed his hand into a rock six days earlier when he dived into a fighting hole as a mortar round landed about 10 yards from him.

"I'm starting to get some numbness in my fingers, but that's about it," Coleman says. "They don't know what's wrong with it. Now, they think it's more of an infection."

Coleman was guarding a Cobra helicopter at a base near Baghdad when the mortar round landed.

"I just dived into my hole. I think God saved my life. I had my sergeant check the back of my flak jacket to make sure I didn't have any shrapnel in there."

After the explosion, he had to stay in the fighting hole to make sure nobody was approaching his line.

"It's war," he says. "You can't let things like that bother you. ... You can't stop what you are doing. You gotta keep moving."

Coleman is a heavy-equipment operator, but he's been used mainly for security.

"Now, when I hear explosions or mortar rounds going off, I get weary about things," he says. "You start hearing noises, and you wonder if it's mortar or not."

He hasn't fired his weapon, but he's faced fire — potshots from civilians — and was unable to return fire. "With a lot of the potshots we are taking, there are too many civilians around," he says. "They take a couple of potshots, and they are gone. A lot of

April 12, 2003

times, you can't fire. They don't want you firing into a crowd because you want to keep peace with the civilians."

Coleman joined the Marine Corps Reserve when he was 19, following in the footsteps of his stepfather, Patrick McKenna. He has been in Iraq for about three weeks and in the Middle East for two months.

"It's been a good experience for me because you'll appreciate America a lot more," he says. "It's an experience nobody should have to live through. It's never pretty, never a nice thing. But it's something we have to do."

April 5, 2003

NAME: Michael Simmons
RANK: Marine sergeant
AGE: 23
HOMETOWN: St. Louis, Mo.
DUTY: Commander of a light armored vehicle, 2nd Marine Division, 2nd
Light Armor Reconnaissance Battalion, Alpha Company, 2nd Platoon

Marine lucky — until the 15th missile

CAMP VIPER, southern Iraq — Marine Sgt. Michael Simmons lies on his back, on a bed in Fleet Hospital No. 3 in southern Iraq, with his right arm above his head. His flak jacket, his lucky one, is thrown on the floor under the bed. A jagged chunk of shrapnel is taped to his dog tags.

Simmons calls his wife.

"I have good news and bad news," Simmons says. It's the first time he's talked to her in two months. They've been married nearly a year.

"All right," Amy Simmons says.

"The good news is that I might be coming home soon," he says.

She is thrilled.

"The bad news is that I got shot," he says.

She starts crying.

"It's not that bad," he says.

Simmons, 23, of St. Louis, Mo., is a vehicle commander for a light armored vehicle, which has eight wheels and looks like a tank. He is in charge of a driver, a gunner and four scouts on the back, who are armed with M16 rifles.

"We were told we were going to do a humanitarian mission on a small town, about 30 kilometers south of Kut, Simmons says. "As we were rolling up there, we got an intelligence report that there may be an ambush up there."

He shrugs. "Pretty much every town we roll into, there might be an ambush."

Simmons is assigned to the 2nd Marine Division, 2nd Light Armor Reconnaissance Battalion, Alpha Company, 2nd Platoon, which is based at Camp Lejuene, N.C.

At the start of the war, his platoon raced through the desert without facing much resistance.

"All we saw was sand and camels," he says. "But the farther north we went, every little town would get worse and worse."

South of Kut, they rolled up to a bridge. "It was outside a little Podunk town," Simmons says. "I don't even know its name."

The road was barricaded, and they started taking rocket-propelled grenade fire.

"Back up," Simmons screamed to his crew.

They retreated about 200 meters.

"We began immediately engaging on the town," Simmons says. "We'd see little muzzle flashes from the small-arms fire and pretty big muzzle flashes from the rocket-propelled grenades."

The commanding officer called for artillery fire, an air strike and Cobra helicopters.

An Iraqi tank started shooting guided missiles at his light armored vehicle. By his count, the Iraqis had launched 14 missiles at his vehicle during the last two weeks, but nothing ever reached it.

"I'm the point vehicle, and it usually takes the brunt of the attack," he says. "I've been lucky up to this point."

Until the 15th missile.

And then the 16th.

All he heard was the explosions. The first missile hit the front of the light armored vehicle, shattering the driver's periscope. The second rocket hit the smoke grenade launcher, mounted on the turret.

A piece of shrapnel entered his right wrist, snapping his hand back and severing an artery. He screamed and blood started sputtering out of his wrist. Simmons looked down and the smoke grenade launcher was on fire.

"I covered up my wrist and told my driver to back up as fast as he can," Simmons says.

The fire concerned him. They were carrying 40 pounds of explosives.

"Shoot at anything that moves," Simmons screamed to the gunner.

As Simmons was put in a company ambulance, he heard the bombers coming in and the artillery start hitting the town.

"The rest of the battalion rolled up," he says. "They gave me thumbs-up as they went by. They told me they were going to take care of it.

"When I was in the field, they sutured it up, not realizing it was an artery. I had a lot of internal bleeding and my arm swelled up over the next day."

Simmons was taken to the fleet hospital in a helicopter and had two surgeries. It was the first fleet hospital set up in Iraq, and Simmons was the first U.S. patient.

"I got the royal treatment," he says. "There were 30 nurses and one patient. I was impressed with this place."

Doctors had to make a cut from his hand to the base of his elbow, to let the blood and swelling drain out.

"It's all open meat," Simmons says. "I got to look at it. You can see all the tendons and muscles."

He looks at his hand. He's a music buff, a guitar player, and he's been assured that he will regain full use of his hand.

"There was a slight chance that the nerve was severed, but the surgeon assures me that it's just bruised," he says. "It will be upwards of five months until I get full use of my hand again."

Simmons didn't realize how lucky he was until he saw his flak jacket. A piece of shrapnel went through two layers of the vest and penetrated a ballistic plate, but stopped halfway through. It was aimed right for the middle of his sternum.

"I'm keeping that vest," he says. "My colonel came up and asked how I was doing. I said, 'Sir, I'm keeping my flak jacket.'

"He said, 'I don't think that will be a problem.'"

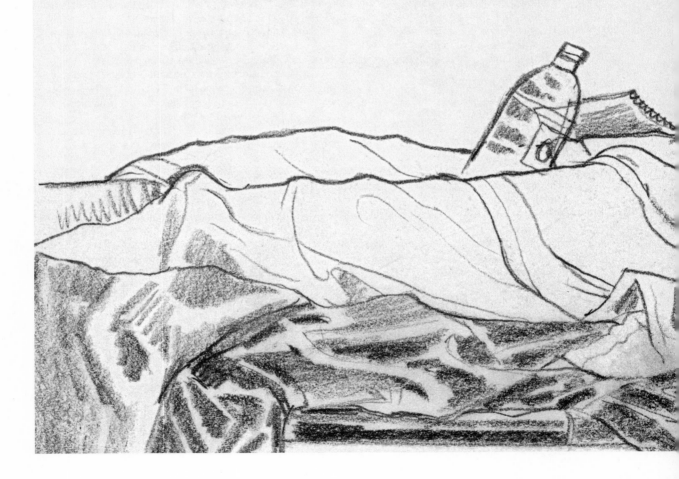

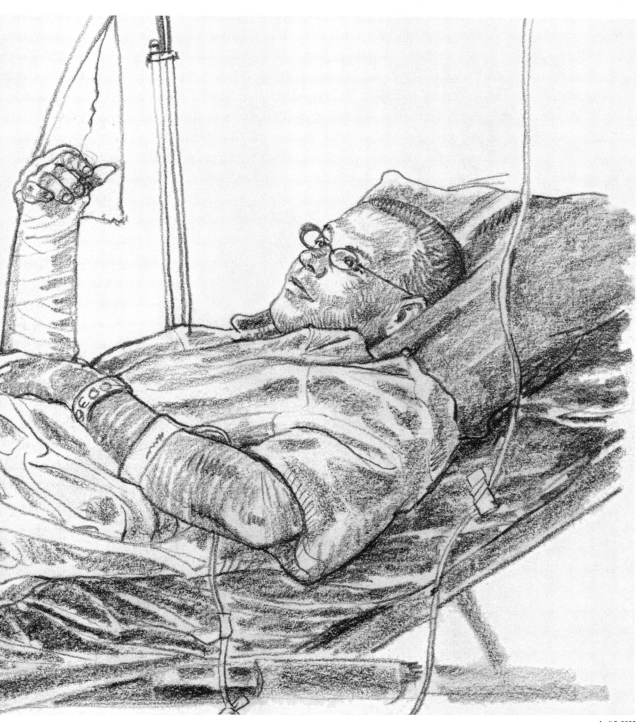

April 5, 2003

April 12, 2003

April 8, 2003

CHAPTER 8

Civilians & Rebuilding: 'I don't know what will happen in Iraq.'

April 11, 2003

Feb. 16, 2003

NAME: Ahmed Almas Al-Sulaiti
AGE: 35
HOMETOWN: Doha, Qatar
DUTY: Commercial officer
at Qatargas, which produces
liquefied natural gas

NAME: Yousef Al-Sulaiti
AGE: 4
HOMETOWN: Doha, Qatar

Qatari man fretful about war, son, job

MANAMA, Bahrain — The child sleeps soundly, peacefully unaware.

His father is nervous. He wants to take his family out of the Middle East, away from the threat of war, but he has nowhere to go. And besides, he has a job to do, supplying the world with natural gas.

So they go about their daily lives.

Ahmed Almas Al-Sulaiti sits in an airport lounge in Manama waiting to get on a plane back to his home in Doha, Qatar. His 4-year-old son, Yousef, sleeps on a couch, the first time he's slept soundly in weeks.

"If the war starts, where should I take my son?" Al-Sulaiti asks. "Where should I go? Everything is going to be closed. Airports? Closed. Where can I take him? I don't want to leave Doha, but I'm concerned about my family. If Saddam Hussein has the biological weapons, yes, I'm concerned about that, but I don't know if he does."

Yousef is still asleep, his head resting on a pillow.

If there is a war in Iraq, U.S. commanders plan to run it from a base in Doha, about 10 miles from where Al-Sulaiti lives.

"I'm glad the Americans are in my country, but I'm not glad with what's happening," he says.

"We don't want war."

The U.S. military is also using an air field in Doha. Journalists have not been allowed onto the base, Al Udeid, because Qatar is trying to minimize its involvement.

"I'm worried about our people, our family, our kids. I am concerned."

But it's not enough to stop his life or his travels.

Al-Sulaiti, 35, took his son to Bahrain to see a dermatologist. Yousef has severe eczema, a skin condition that causes dry skin and intense itching. Yousef's prescription ran out two weeks ago, and he's been miserable since. He and his father have been to several doctors in Qatar but have found only one medicine that alleviates the problem. The only place they can get it is in Bahrain.

"He cannot sleep for two weeks," Al-Sulaiti says. "He's crying all day long. I wanted the doctor to see him, and maybe she will change the medicine. Within three days, he'll be OK."

Al-Sulaiti was able to get a three-month supply.

But what will happen in those three months?

And what will happen to his work?

Al-Sulaiti is one of two commercial officers at Qatargas, which pioneered liquefied natural gas production in Qatar. The country of Qatar owns the gas, but Qatargas is one of several companies that transport it.

"I'm in charge of all the ships and invoice them," Al-Sulaiti says. "We have 11 ships. I'm in charge of the documents, distribution, contact with the buyers, doing the invoices."

One ship can transport $14 million to $15 million worth of product, he says. Qatargas supplies natural gas to power companies in Japan, Spain, Turkey, Italy, South Korea, Britain and the United States. Qatargas' goal is bold: to become the world's leading supplier of natural gas.

"If there is a war, it will slow business dramatically," Al-Sulaiti says, "because buyers will be reluctant to fly to Qatar to sign a contract. If there is a war, there will be no buyers."

It is a 45-minute flight from Bahrain to Qatar. Yousef, a thin, tender boy with big brown eyes full of innocence, sits in a giant seat in business class, swinging his legs, playing with his father's cell phone. He playfully sticks out his tongue at a reporter, sitting across the aisle.

Yousef seems happy and content, after weeks of suffering.

"He's too young to understand," Al-Sulaiti says. "Nobody wants war. Nobody needs war. There are too many wars."

March 5, 2003

NAME: Fahad Dousari
AGE: 25
HOMETOWN: Kuwait City
JOB: Oil field engineer in Kuwait

Cousin may be prisoner of Iraq — or dead

BURGAN OIL FIELD, Kuwait — Fahad Dousari remembers the fires, how the afternoon sky turned black with oily smoke.

He remembers walking through Kuwait City and being stopped at gunpoint by the Iraqi military, terrified and dehumanized.

And he remembers his cousin, Khaled Dousari — how they used to play basketball and soccer together. "He was tall and he is serious," Fahad Dousari says, unconsciously mixing tenses, unsure exactly how to refer to him.

"I don't know if he's dead or alive."

Khaled Dousari may be one of 605 prisoners of war from Kuwait being held in Iraq for more than 10 years, according to Kuwaiti accusations.

Iraqi officials have rejected the charges.

"Some people say he's still there in Iraq," Dousari says. "We have some sources in Iraq, people who came out of Iraq, and they told us he is still there — but we haven't heard anything from him."

The POWs were taken during the Iraqi occupation of Kuwait from Aug. 2, 1990, to Feb. 26, 1991.

"Some of them were taken because they were military personnel," says Fawaz Bourisly, media researcher for the Kuwait Ministry of Information. "Some were taken from the mosques in the night. Some were taken from their homes. Some were accused of working with the Kuwaiti resistance, so they took them. Some of them, they didn't disclose. Most of them were working with the Kuwaiti resistance."

Dousari holds out hope that his cousin is alive.

"Maybe they are using them as cards to negotiate," he says.

Dousari, 25, was a teenager when Iraq invaded Kuwait. "I remember the whole war," he says. "How they destroyed Kuwait. How they treated us. They didn't have human decency."

After staying in Kuwait for two months during

March 5, 2003

Iraqi occupation, Dousari and his family escaped to Saudi Arabia. His cousin stayed.

Khaled Dousari, who is 37 if he's alive, was a member of the Kuwaiti military.

"He was in the marines, but he was taken as a civilian," Fahed Dousari says.

When Dousari and his family returned after the war, their house was still standing but "everything was stolen," Dousari says.

"Thank God, the most important thing was that we had a country. You can live in a tent; you can live anywhere, if you have a country."

Dousari studied for five years in the United

States, graduating with an electrical engineering degree from California State University in Los Angeles. For the last two years, he has been an engineer for the government-owned Kuwait Oil Co. at Burgan Oil Field, the world's second-largest oil field.

Now, it's early March 2003, and the company is preparing for war, implementing safety precautions in case Iraq tries to destroy the oil fields again.

In 1991, as allied forces liberated Kuwait, Iraq set Burgan Oil Field on fire. At one point, 700 wells burned in Kuwait, leaving the sky pitch black during the day.

A couple miles from Dousari's office, the destruction remains at Gathering Center No. 14. The ground is scorched black for hundreds of yards. Huge oil storage containers are crushed and crippled from the intense heat from the fire. Crumpled, twisted, broken pipes rise into the air.

But on the edge of Gathering Center No. 14, where the black ground turns into rocky sand, yellow dandelions have popped up.

Life on the fringes.

Swaying in the wind.

"Nobody wants war," Dousari says. "We just want to get rid of Saddam Hussein. That's what we want."

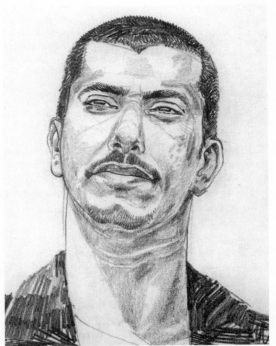

March 5, 2003

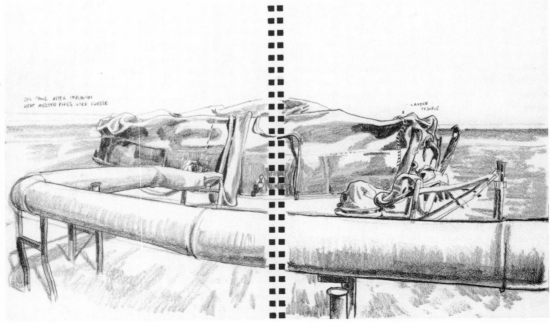

March 5, 2003

GATEWAY TO THE DESTROYED
OIL WELLS NEAR KUWAIT CITY

March 5, 2003

MOHAMMAD

April 8, 2003

NAME: Mohammad
AGE: 32
HOMETOWN: Nasiriyah, Iraq
DUTY: Teacher

Iraqi teacher sees war everywhere

EAST OF NASIRIYAH, Iraq — The teacher sees his young students in the streets, looking at the shattered windows and destroyed buildings, and he tries to comfort them.

"How are you?" he asks.

"We are afraid," the children reply.

"Don't be afraid," the teacher says. "Sit in your home. Don't go in the road."

Mohammad, who asked that his full name not be used because he fears retribution from supporters of Iraqi President Saddam Hussein, has been a teacher for seven years in Nasiriyah. He works with children at the elementary school level, mostly 6- and 7-year-olds.

They haven't had school in more than two weeks since the fighting began. Nasiriyah is now controlled by U.S. forces.

"Maybe, if they go to school, they die because an explosion comes," he says. "I teach 14 children, 14 babies."

He stands outside a U.S. Army hospital, wearing sandals, blue dress pants and a blue dress shirt. He brought his father here for treatment.

"My father hasn't eaten for two days," Mohammad says. He points to his head. "I think it's shock from the bombings. Now, he's very sick. Too much explosions. Too much bombs."

Mohammad stands in the doorway, hoping to hear some news about what is wrong with his father. He waits with two brothers, a cousin and a neighbor.

Mohammad says the people in his city don't have electricity or running water. And their food supply is running low.

"We take water from the river and then put it over a fire," Mohammad says. "We need fresh tomatoes and meat."

Mohammad and 12 relatives live together in a home in Nasiriyah. He has three children.

"The little children are crying all night," Moham-

April 8, 2003

mad says. "They are afraid all the time. They don't go out of the house. They are afraid some bomb will kill them."

A bomb, or perhaps a missile, landed outside his neighbor's house. The neighbor went outside to check on the damage, and another landed on the house, destroying it. The neighbor wasn't hurt.

Mohammad couldn't sleep for three days because of ringing in his ears.

"We have war with Iran for eight years," Mohammad says. "I don't see any bomb in my area. It was away from me. After that, we have war with Kuwait. I think for three months, until America came to

WAITING AT
TALIL HOSPITAL.

April 8, 2003

Kuwait. I don't see any weapons in my neighborhood. In this war, I see weapons."

He doesn't see any Iraqi soldiers in the streets of his city anymore, just American soldiers in Humvees.

The fighting has subsided in his city, but the fears are constant. Mohammad says he has heard about an explosive that drops from a bomb and hits the ground, sounding like a crying baby.

"When you go to see what's the matter, it explodes," he says. "Some neighbors tell me when he hears his mother crying, he won't go and see her."

The Marines say they are not familiar with such a bomb.

"I don't know what will happen in Iraq," Mohammad says. "I hope it's finished. We need to go back to working and teaching and need to live life."

Mohammad's brother, who asked to remain anonymous, says he is happy to see the American troops. "Of course, we are happy that America come here," he says. "We want good future. We don't know what will happen. We don't know what America will do. We don't know what tomorrow will bring in this country."

A doctor comes outside to talk to the family.

"Your father is going to be staying overnight," he says.

"OK," Mohammad says.

"We will try to get his energy up as much as possible, giving him fluids," the doctor says. "Then, you'll pick him up tomorrow."

Tomorrow.

For a change, the word sounds hopeful to Mohammad.

"It's up to God," he says.

April 11, 2003

Humanity breaks through uncertainty

CAMP CHESTY, central Iraq — An intelligence report comes over the radio: An unknown number of Iraqi military might be hiding in a small village, near Camp Chesty in central Iraq.

Sgt. T.R. Sparenberg is on security patrol with his squad. It's his responsibility to check it out.

Sparenberg tells the Marines in his squad to put bayonets on their M16 rifles.

"I gave the order to fix bayonets, so the knives couldn't be pulled off of us," Sparenberg says. "Also, I figured we wouldn't have to take time to do it while going into the village."

Worried about an ambush, Sparenberg decides to enter the village from the rear. But there's a problem as they approach on foot. They come up to a creek filled with knee-high water.

"I wanted to keep the guys' feet dry as long as possible," Sparenberg says. "I'm the only one who stumbled and went waist deep."

PVT. SCOTT REYLING starts to cross the creek.

Three months ago, he never dreamed that he would be in the Marines, much less Iraq.

Reyling joined the Marine Reserve five years ago. About 1½ years ago, he went through a crisis in his life and wanted to make several changes. "I was pretty depressed," he says. He met with officials at the Marine Reserve and thought he was discharged.

He stopped going to drills, but the paperwork was never completed.

When the 6th Engineer Support Battalion was activated Jan. 14, officials realized the mistake. Reyling was forced to return to the battalion or face federal charges. Several Marines went to his office and escorted him back into Marine life.

He had so much military background that he was able to quickly adjust, although he was out of shape.

"I'm glad that I can go back and finish what I started," he says.

He crosses the river and heads toward the village.

THE MARINES SPREAD OUT, about 50 paces apart, marching toward the village.

They can see houses up on the far left.

Lance Cpl. Curtis Wayne isn't nervous. He reacts on instinct.

"For me, it's not a big deal, just because we train for it," he says. "It's almost to the point where everything you have learned to this point has taken over. You don't think. You just react."

Wayne enjoys the Marine Reserve because there is so much at stake. In the real world, he works as a carpenter, building custom homes.

"In the Marines, if you aren't on your toes, you'll end up in the hospital," he says. "I like that aspect of it. I like knowing if I screw up, it won't be good. I'll end up in a hospital."

LANCE CPL. IRA ROY ALLEN, 20, moves quickly through the tall, lush, green grass.

He joined the Marine Corps in October 1999.

"I've always been fascinated by the Marine Corps," he says. "I was the short, fat kid in high school. I didn't have a lot of confidence."

He weighed almost 200 pounds in junior high school. "I was a little porker," he says. "In the Marines, I found I could push myself harder than I thought I could."

Now, he weighs about 160 pounds. "I'm a lot happier when I look at myself," he says.

Allen, a Marine reservist, attends a technical institute near Chicago, Ill., studying automotive and diesel program.

"I've always been interested in cars," he says. "I like working on cars. When I get back, I want to get an engineering degree, more towards designing them. I like the technology and electronics."

**Marine Lance
Corporal Ira Roy
Allen on patrol.**

April 11, 2003

April 11, 2003

April 11, 2003

MOVING THROUGH THE FIELD, Cpl. Andrew Szostak feels like he is in another war. "It felt like we were in Vietnam," he says.

Szostak, 26, studies mechanical engineering at Bradley University in Peoria, Ill.

He was raised in a family with nine children. "I was top of the bottom four," he says.

He was 20 when he joined the service, following in the footsteps of his father and three uncles. He has one year left as a reservist, and he's not sure if he's going to re-up.

SPARENBERG IS SURPRISED when they approach the village and nobody is around. They see several buildings and animal pens.

"I'll be damned, they didn't know we were there," Sparenberg says. "We actually surprised them. They were shocked when we showed up."

They line up across the entrance to the village, spread out, along the edge of the field.

Now, the Iraqis know the Marines have arrived.

Sparenberg asks a man to come forward. The man, who looks pleased to see Sparenberg, is holding a radio. Sparenberg asks him to put the radio down and Wayne searches him.

Sparenberg tries to communicate with the Iraqis without talking. "I started asking them questions pointing at a card instead of talking," he says. "If somebody was there, it could give it away."

He points to a phrase, enemy soldier.

"No," they say in broken English.

THE MARINES START to search the houses.

"We weren't supposed to do it really dynamic because we didn't want to scare them too bad," Lance Cpl. John Alvarado says. "I went in half speed. We would walk in and there would be women and children huddled in the corner. The children were

Sgt. T.R. Sparenberg on patrol.

March 23, 2003

usually crying. There was nothing there."

Many of the women have tattoos on their faces, hands and arms. "In the back of my head, I didn't think there would be people there," Alvarado says. "I was more afraid I would pop in and there would be a civilian. The women and children acted like they didn't like us.

"I felt bad because I was going into their houses. There were a lot of rugs on the floor. There would be a really nice TV and a crappy pot that they were cooking food in. I didn't step on their rugs. I had muddy boots."

April 11, 2003

THE STRESS QUICKLY MELTS away and everyone starts taking pictures and shaking hands.

Sparenberg meets a man with one eye, a hole in his foot and a scar on his chest. "Saddam," the man says, pointing to the injuries.

Sparenberg sits down with an Iraqi, puts his rifle on his lap and offers him a cigarette.

They sit side by side, two guys, posing for a picture.

For Sparenberg, it is an amazing moment, a chance to build some bridges.

"We got to know them after we secured the area," Sparenberg says. "I met the children. I love children. We wanted to let them know we were there to protect them. They were not our enemy. We were there to protect them.

"Most of the talking was done with hands. I would point to the children, or wave my hand and put a smile on my face. I said children make me smile. I told them they were God's gift. They were getting what we were trying to say, and then we were trying to pick up what they were trying to say. They were all male. None of the women or daughters came out."

They spend about 30 minutes in the village. "It gave everybody an uplifting spirit," Sparenberg says.

Somehow, in the middle of a war, the humanity broke through on both sides. The Iraqis risked standing in front of the Marines. And the Marines took a risk, putting down their firearms.

As they left, the villagers stood in the front of the village and waved.

"It was a Time Life magazine cover where everybody is waving good-bye," Sparenberg says.

After leaving the village, Sparenberg pulls his

April 11, 2003

Marines into a tight group, in a secured area, between two berms.

"I think we just gave them a better outlook on the United States Marine Corps," Sparenberg says. "Coming out of that village, I've never seen so many smiles. There was definitely an upbeat feeling, which is great for them. It was good for me. I wanted to let them know we weren't there to harm them."

April 11, 2003

NAME: Ira Roy Allen

RANK: Marine lance corporal

AGE: 20

HOMETOWN: Springfield, Vt.

DUTY: Combat engineer

April 11, 2003

NAME: Andrew Szostak

RANK: Marine corporal

AGE: 26

HOMETOWN:
Bolingbrook, Ill.

DUTY: Combat
engineer, 6th Engineer
Support Battalion

NAME: Curtis Wayne
RANK: Marine lance corporal
AGE: 22
HOMETOWN: Weldon, Ill.
DUTY: Combat engineer, 6th Engineer Support Battalion

April 11, 2003

NAME: Scott Reyling
RANK: Marine private
AGE: 23
HOMETOWN: Peoria, Ill.
DUTY: Combat engineer, 6th Engineer Support Battalion

April 11, 2003

April 11, 2003

April 12, 2003

NAME: Rusty Miller
RANK: Marine master gunnery sergeant
AGE: 43
HOMETOWN: Ida, Mich.
DUTY: Runs the Combat Operations Center
for the 6th Engineer Support Battalion

Iraqi crowd gathers, but will it shoot weapons or smiles?

NUMANIYAH, Iraq — Master Gunnery Sgt. Rusty Miller sits in a Humvee, riding through a small town in central Iraq, wearing a flak jacket and Kevlar helmet. He has no idea what's going to happen. Will the Iraqis shoot weapons or smiles?

The war has entered a strange stage: Most of the fighting is done, but it's still a dangerous situation.

The six-vehicle convoy is heavily protected by a security force armed with machine guns. It moves quickly through the outskirts of Numaniyah, a town on the banks of the Tigris. The main street is bustling with hundreds of Iraqis, standing on sidewalks, shopping at an outdoor market, buying vegetables.

The scene reminds Miller of Okinawa, Japan, where he spent seven years earlier in his career.

"In Okinawa, all the people gather around, and they have the vegetable markets and all that and the little shops," Miller says. "Everybody just kind of wanders and barters."

But this is Iraq.

And everything is still tenuous.

The Iraqis stand and stare at the Americans. Most wave or give a thumbs-up.

But what does it mean?

In many ways, the Iraqis have no choice but to stop and wave. It keeps them alive. When you travel down a highway in Iraq, every time you pass a civilian vehicle, the Iraqis smile and wave to the U.S. military. But you have no idea whether it's genuine.

The convoy passes a defaced picture of Saddam Hussein. Children ride bikes, and a donkey pulls a wagon, filled with children.

The convoy makes a wrong turn, down a two-lane road, and children run up to the convoy, trying to chase it down. Most are barefoot. Trash and paper are scattered along the ground on both sides of the road. It looks like a storm has gone through town.

The Marines notice black flags hanging on buildings. Some of the Marines have been told that means the people inside are supporters of Hussein; other Marines have been told the color black is symbolic of mourning and death.

The convoy comes to a stop, along the banks of the Tigris. An old empty hull is beached on sand, sticking up in the air. The Marines get out of their vehicles and are swarmed by about 75 Iraqis, all males, including many children.

Miller picks up a child and poses for a picture.

Miller is smiling, the boy is smiling, and everyone seems thrilled. The children appear to be genuinely happy to see the Americans. Miller has three children of his own: Christian Michael, 22; Jacob, 12, and Kylee, 6.

"It's like when you go to a carnival and you see something special, like the lion tamer," he says. "That's what it felt like."

Most of the children don't speak English, but they are able to communicate. Miller shows a group of children a trick with his fingers, tapping them up and down, making one seem to disappear, and they laugh.

"They wanted money," Miller says. "They don't know what money is. I had candy. And I wanted to give them candy, but there were so many of them that if you would have given them some, they would have been all over you. So you couldn't do that."

Miller pats a child on the head. "Where are your shoes?" Miller asks.

A man who speaks broken English tells Miller: "He doesn't own any."

Miller is hit with a wave of sadness, if not guilt, but then he snaps out of it.

Opposite: A girl peeks at Marines through a backyard gate in Numaniyah, Iraq.

April 12, 2003

"Look at where they live," he says. "It doesn't snow or anything. Their feet are filthy, just like mine were in the country as a little kid."

MILLER WAS RAISED on a farm in Ida, Mich. He joined the Marine Corps the day after Thanksgiving in 1977.

"I joined because my friend did," he says. "I didn't want to work on a farm or in a factory. Everybody wanted to go to Chevy or Chrysler. I didn't want to work in a factory the rest of my life. It's good money, but they were all dirty or nasty when you first got in, until you got your seniority and stuff. I just couldn't see myself doing that."

Miller spent three years on active duty and then got out.

"I was getting a divorce at the time," he says. "I got frustrated with it. I was a farm boy from Michigan, and it wasn't for me. I got out and moved to Washington, D.C., because all my buddies were still in. After a year, I decided to come back in. Then, I've been back ever since."

Miller has spent time at Camp Pendleton, Calif.; Okinawa; Quantico, Va., and Cuba.

"It's been exciting," Miller says. "I got to travel a lot of places. Sometimes, it's been frustrating with the Marine Corps not having a lot of money, when you see the other services with the new equipment, new barracks and stuff like that. But all in all, I'd do it again."

He was supposed to go on leave March 28 and retire June 30.

"I kind of had my choice. But if I would have wanted out, I would have needed real good justification. I'm the only one in my job within the battalion with no replacement. So I said I would stay."

Miller runs the Combat Operations Center for the 6th Engineer Support Battalion. Most times, he couldn't feel any farther from home.

April 12, 2003

"In Ida, there are cornfields everywhere," he says. "We got a flashing red light about 20 years ago for the first time. It's a real small community. My senior class had like 80 people who graduated in it."

Miller, a hunting and fishing fanatic, gets home to Michigan a couple of times a year to visit his parents, Alton and Sharon Miller.

"They still have the farm that I was raised on," he says. "It's 150 years old. All my brothers and sisters live there. I'm the only one who left."

When he retires, it looks like he will work in military acquisition in Virginia.

THE CROWD CONTINUES TO GROW: It's mostly children and older people.

"Money," the children say. "Money."

Miller reaches into his pockets and the kids swarm around him. He pulls out the bottom of an empty pocket, to try to show them he doesn't have anything.

He rubs their heads and pats them on the back.

"Hi," he says, loudly. And then he laughs. "Of course, you always talk to them like they are deaf," he says. "We always do that with foreign people, like they can't hear. It's not that they can't hear. It's that they can't understand."

He meets a man with 80 cents in change. "He wanted some more," Miller says. "I was trying to explain to him that one more quarter was a dollar. I went into the truck and got a quarter. When I shook his hand good-bye, I gave him a quarter."

It's one of the wildest scenes he's ever seen.

"I'm from Michigan," Miller says. "Where am I ever going to see something like that?"

Security tries to keep the Iraqis back, away from the Humvees. "They are waving at you, and they are friendly, so you hope they are nice," Miller says. But it's also scary at times.

"You hear all the reports and read about them on the computer, how they are attacking you.

"Are they happy you are here? Or because Saddam is gone? Or because you are going to give them some food and candy? You don't know why they are happy. But I don't think the kids are acting. All kids are innocent."

The security team notices a group of Iraqis approaching in an expensive car. It looks like three men in their late teens or early 20s. The Marines have been briefed on suicide bombers and Iraqis who take potshots. Security decides to load up the vehicles.

As Miller gets into a Humvee, a man asks for water for his baby. Miller can't give him any. A small boy runs behind the Humvee as the convoy leaves, and Miller throws him some candy.

As the convoy leaves town, the Iraqis wave and smile — and give thumbs-up.

**Hasnam
Osman**

April 12, 2003

NAMES: Aman, Sumeya and Hasnam Osman
HOMETOWN: Numaniyah, Iraq

Family's gesture benefits whole town

NUMANIYAH, Iraq — Iraqi soldiers were outside the house, hiding in the bushes.

"Until two weeks ago, they were there," Sumeya Osman says, motioning to the thick shrubs and trees behind the one-story brick house on the banks of the Tigris.

"Very afraid, we were," she says.

After the United States invaded Iraq, the Iraqi soldiers left, taking along a power grid that ran the town generator.

When the Marines moved nearby — building a base along the canals, drawing water for forward units — people from the town complained.

But the Marines gave them a generator so they could maintain their water supply.

"I'm thankful," Aman Osman says, through his cousin, Sumeya Osman, who speaks broken English and acts as his interpreter.

Aman Osman's job is to supply water to farmers in the area. He lives in the small house along the Tigris, with his wife and seven children. His children left town and stayed with Sumeya Osman during the initial stages of the war.

"There were bombs for a month," says Sumeya Osman. "Nobody died. Everybody was OK."

At the end of the road, two Iraqi trucks are left, destroyed under a bridge. About a quarter-mile away, two more Iraqi military vehicles are blown to bits. The ground is covered with metal and shards of glass.

"At night, there is no one walking the streets,"

Aman Osman says. He stands with his 8-year-old daughter, Hasnam, wrapping his arms around her.

"Saddam was a leader of our country, and now he is gone," Aman Osman says to an American journalist. "For you, I am happy."

The generator that the Marines let him borrow worked for a while before it conked out. They have returned to fix it.

As one group of Marines works on the generator, Aman Osman invites another group into his house. As they enter, four women rush into the kitchen without speaking. Their faces are covered.

The room is dark and empty.

"This is the food room," Sumeya Osman says, "where we are drinking and eating food."

Aman Osman invites the group into his bedroom. There is a queen-size bed with a blanket. There are no chairs or pictures on the walls. A single dresser with a mirror stands in the corner. Against the wall, there is a closet filled with sheets and blankets.

A large rug covers the tile floor.

Two windows face the Tigris. Chickens walk around the backyard.

"We want a government that will supply us with water, with food and peace," Aman Osman says.

Lt. Col. Roger Machut, who is in charge of the 6th Engineer Support Battalion, is outside as Marines work on the generator. After about 15 minutes, the generator is working again. The small town has power, which means the family has water.

Aman Osman shakes Machut's hand.

Sumeya Osman (Aman's cousin).

April 12, 2003

AMAN OSMAN

Aman Osman (Hasnam's father).

April 12, 2003

April 12, 2003

Iraqi kids touch troops' hearts

ON THE ROAD TO BAGHDAD — They stand by the side of the road, waving at the convoys.

Hundreds of Iraqi children.

As thousands of Marines and soldiers head north toward Baghdad, in massive convoys that snake to the horizon — trucks and Humvees and tankers, filled with equipment and supplies and reinforcements — the children line the route through the desert.

Some hold empty water bottles, begging for a drink.

Many just stand and smile, some with a look of apprehension, others with joy and excitement.

Most hold up Iraqi money, wanting to trade for American cash. For $1, you get an old crumpled bill featuring Saddam Hussein's face.

The children are dirty and look tired. Almost all are barefoot, walking on the hot sand and gravel.

They try to communicate, using deliberate gestures. A little boy in a white flowing gown, tattered and flowing in the breeze, taps his mouth and then pats his belly.

Over and over.

Others just hold out both hands, palms up, hopeful and eager, looking desperate.

Only a handful have parents with them.

The trucks drive by, going about 45 miles per hour, and the kids are left in a cloud of dust. At times, on the wrong side of the wind, they become almost invisible.

But other times, there are so many military vehicles, on one road, at one time, heading into the fight, that it turns into a massive traffic jam.

The trucks come to a stop, and you can hear the voices of the children: "Mistah!"

"Money, money."

At the site of a nasty firefight just a few days earlier, about 80 children stand by the side of the road, holding up blue boxes of Iraqi cigarettes.

The Marines call it gasoline alley: "Every time you go through there at night, you get filled up with lead."

But daylight brings out the children.

Four are selling bottles of Pepsi.

A boy holds up a Playboy magazine, a gift, apparently, from an American soldier. The Marines laugh and shower him with candy, as he flashes them pictures of pinups.

"Smart kid," somebody says.

The Marines have been told not to give the children any food or water. It only creates chaos, as the children swarm the trucks. As the Marines say, if you give a child a bottle of water, there's no way to be sure he or she will be the one who gets to drink it.

But you can't help it.

STAFF SGT. JEREMY WESTLAKE of Charlie Company, 6th Engineer Support Battalion, sees a tender little girl in a purple dress. Barefoot. Sad eyes. Dark hair. She looks like an angel, full of innocence.

He tosses her a piece of candy, and it whizzes by her head. He feels bad — but glad it didn't hit her. He's a hard-charging Marine. An expert with just about every gun in the Marine Corps.

For weeks, he hasn't shown a soft side.

Until now.

The next day, Westlake sees the girl again, on the trip back south to Camp Viper, and he can't get her out of his head.

"How do I go about adopting an Iraqi?" he asks. "I could put her in my sea bag and take her home with me. She's just adorable."

A BOY STANDS OUTSIDE an empty brick building about the size of a two-car garage. It doesn't have windows or a door, just a flat roof that bakes in the sunshine. He wears a brown shirt, torn at the bottom. He stands without moving, as a giant convoy of

April 12, 2003

Marines goes past. He holds up his left thumb and smiles.

I point at him, and he smiles even harder.

Is he hungry?

Where are his parents?

What will become of him?

What will become of his country?

He's about 3 years old, with dark eyes and a big smile, just like my youngest child.

Our convoy keeps moving, keeps pushing forward. The boy is long gone, but I keep thinking about him, wishing I could do something more. I see more children, and after a while, it gets so sad, so depressing, I can't look anymore.

April 8, 2003

NAME: Mohammed Alsalahi

AGE: 36

HOMETOWN: Born in Nasiriyah, Iraq, but lives in San Diego, Calif.

DUTY: Works for the Iraqi Free Officer and Civilian Movement

Iraqi returns to help mend ties and nation

EAST OF NASIRIYAH, Iraq — Mohammed Alsalahi stands outside a U.S. Army hospital, trying to help translate for a group of Iraqi men who don't speak English.

"His brother died, and they want the body back," Alsalahi tells an Army nurse, who speaks only English.

The body has been buried.

"They want to take him and do Islamic procedures for burial," Alsalahi says.

Alsalahi, 36, of San Diego works with the Iraqi Free Officer and Civilian Movement. He was born and raised in Nasiriyah but left Iraq eight years ago.

He declines to discuss the exact nature of his business in Iraq.

"We are a peace mission," he says. "We are trying to rebuild the relationship between Iraqi people and the United States. It's been destroyed by Saddam and the Baath Party. The main thing is for people to get rid of Saddam and his regime. I am part of this mission. We are here to participate with the allies to liberate our country."

He wears camouflage military fatigues and a flak jacket, and he carries a pistol.

"I left Iraq because of Saddam, because of the situation here," he says. "I come back here to liberate our country. I'm living here, at this base. We will help rebuild Iraq with our friends in America."

A nurse returns to speak to the Iraqi men about trying to get the body.

"They use civilians as human shields, and that's how this happens," Alsalahi says. "He was with his brothers and got shot. His brother is now wounded here at the hospital. The other brother died, and they want the body. I know with the Koran, there is a specific way they have to bury the body. They have to read some specific words from the Koran."

Alsalahi is more than a translator. He says he came to this hospital on other matters that he declines to discuss, and he's just helping out.

"I cannot leave them without helping," he says.

Alsalahi has a bachelor's degree in management from a university in Baghdad. He has a wife and two children.

"I'm a student in San Diego," he says.

He's been a member of the organization for three years.

"Our goal is to topple Saddam," Alsalahi says. "It's going to happen. It makes me so happy, so happy I cannot describe it. But our feeling goes between happiness and sorrow that some people have accidentally died."

April 4, 2003

NAME: Roger Machut
RANK: Marine lieutenant colonel
AGE: 42
HOMETOWN: Schaumburg, Ill.
DUTY: Commander of the 6th Engineer Support
Battalion, in charge of 1,586 Marines in Iraq

Battalion gets fuel lifeline flowing

CAMP VIPER, southern Iraq — It all fits, one piece aligning with the next, from President George W. Bush to a single tank in the desert.

But before you can understand this war and see it in a different light, why the military was able to push through Iraq so quickly and why so few Americans died. ...

Before you can understand how Iraq will be rebuilt, starting with essentials like power and water, before a new government can be established. ...

You have to see everything from a different point of view, on a small scale, starting with a simple rubber hose in the desert.

That hose was put together by more than 1,500 Marine reservists, men and women with everyday jobs — teachers, police officers and truck drivers; your next-door neighbors from Portland, Ore., to Peoria, Ill. — united in the desert to build a fuel supply line for the entire 1st Marine Expeditionary Force, pumping diesel to 50,000 Marines for trucks, tanks and helicopters on the front lines. Before you can understand that hose, however, you have to understand the man behind the hose — Lt. Col. Roger Machut, a thin man with a stiff personality, a full-time civil engineer and a part-time Marine, commanding a battalion of reservists.

And to understand the man behind the hose, you have to start with a grenade, during a deadly ambush in Vietnam. That changed everything. That started everything.

It all fits together.

One dot. Then another dot. And another. Until finally, they all come together in a straight line through the desert, forming a hose stretching 57 miles long, capable of pumping a half-million gallons of diesel fuel every day, from Kuwait to Iraq, an artery into the heart of enemy territory, linking different kinds of people and fueling a different kind of war.

To understand what will happen over the next few months — how this man is going to help restore Iraq, in his own small way, giving the people water and power, helping to rebuild roads and buildings, to fix what was so quickly torn down — you have to go back to that grenade.

The day his hero died.

MACHUT WAS 7 WHEN his older brother, Richard, was killed by a grenade in an ambush in Vietnam.

"He was my idol, a Marine, 14½ years older than me," Machut says. "He was on patrol, and they were ambushed. He took a grenade round to the mid-portion of his body. It blew his legs off, basically from the waist down. We were told he didn't suffer long. He lived about a half-hour after that. I remember it all ... being informed, seeing my parents, waiting two weeks for him to come home and the three-day wake.

"I remember those days distinctly. I've lived with his memory and wanted to be like him."

When Machut graduated from high school, there was no question what he was going to do — join the Marines, just like his older brother. He went to see a recruiter, intending to enlist, but the recruiter talked him into going to college and becoming an officer.

Machut went to Tulane University in New Orleans on a Marine scholarship and studied civil engineering. He spent 4½ years on active duty and joined the Marine Corps Reserve in 1988, assigned to the 4th Bridge Company in Battle Creek, Mich.

After bouncing up the ranks, Machut took over the 6th Engineer Support Battalion in September.

"Never in my wildest dreams when I went to Battle Creek as a young captain did I think I would command this battalion, much less command it in war," he says. "I look back on my career and wonder how the heck I ended up here. I can only think it's fate. I was meant to be here."

A few hours before the start of the war, Machut looked like death. His face was cold and pale, focused but tired. There was so much that could go wrong.

The mission sounded simple enough — put down a hose through the middle of the desert and pump diesel fuel 57 miles from Kuwait to a fuel farm in southern Iraq. A fuel farm is like a giant gas station in the desert, only the diesel is stored in huge bladders. Tankers come from the front line, fill up with fuel and take it back to the tanks and trucks.

Sounds simple.

But there were doubters.

"There are some naysayers out there in the Marine Corps who said this has never been done," Machut says. "You can't do it, especially a reserve battalion."

The Marines had never pumped fuel such a long distance, so deep into enemy territory. And if this battalion failed, the supply line would crumble.

The mission couldn't start until the area was secured.

On the second day of the war, Machut heard some disturbing news. The Marines on the front line were starving for fuel, and his battalion was still behind the border.

"I went down and talked to the Marines and told them this is what's at stake," Machut says. "I told them, 'It's Marines your age, from your hometowns, who are literally dying in gunfights. They need air support. They need the accompanying fire from tanks and LAVs,' " which stands for light armored vehicles.

" 'The tanks are having trouble getting up there because they need fuel. The air support needs fuel.' They were going to run out soon."

So they started the mission earlier than expected.

Two companies laid the hose. A third company went forward and started to build the fuel farm in the desert.

Other Marines worked as flank security, protecting the convoys while the trail was marked.

The project was finished ahead of schedule.

"We said four days, and we did it in three days," Machut says. "We did it without the communications support we needed. We did it without the logistical lift that we needed. We started in the middle of the night, as opposed to the middle of the day. On top of that, we set this up in the worst sandstorm in 20 years for this area.

"Lots of things changed. The route changed. The breach through the Kuwaiti berm wasn't where we originally anticipated it would be. As we ran up here, we ran into oil fields that we knew about, but we didn't know the condition of the pipes. We had to adjust for that. There were farms we went through. Our recon unit, which I was a part of, had to figure out a route in order to minimize the length of the hose that was gonna be used."

A WEEK AFTER the hose was put down — an overwhelming success — Machut continued to have concerns. There was no way to protect a soft hose, about 6 inches wide, that stretched for miles across the Iraqi desert.

"Our biggest concern is a guy on a camel with a rusty machete," he says.

One person could have crippled the entire project for a time by cutting the hose.

"The hose reel is a soft target," Machut says. "Right now, there is some idea that there is some enemy trying to infiltrate our rear areas. We've had some sightings of people looking at our stuff. We aren't sure if the hose reel is under watch by bad guys or bedouins who are curious. It's so hard to tell the difference between the two. So far, we haven't had any attacks on the hose reel."

In a strange way, it's been easier for Machut to be in Iraq and lead a battalion into combat than to live his normal life, trying to balance a full-time job as a civil engineer with his family and his military work.

"I put in about 45 to 50 hours a week in my civilian job," Machut says. "I put in 2 to 3 hours a day with the battalion. Then, I try to fit in the other things. A lot of my battalion work is done after the kids go to sleep — after violin lessons and diving practice and everything else. That's a sacrifice of my sleep, to run the battalion."

Machut and his wife, Linda, have two children.

"A lot of ways, I think I'm fortunate that I've been mobilized," he says. "As much as I miss my family, as much as an impact as it is on my civilian job, I can't be involved with them right now. ... The only thing I have to do is worry about my battalion."

In early April, the weather was starting to get warm in the desert, but Machut continued to wear a black fleece hat borrowed from his 15-year-old son, Dan.

"I took it from home when I came over in January," Machut says. "I knew I'd be cold. I still wear it today, even though the weather is getting warmer. As weird as it sounds, I wear it because not only does it keep me warm, but I think my son keeps me warm."

Machut brought along a photo album, put together by his daughter, Lindsay, 11.

Machut is an associate partner for a 90-person engineering firm in Itasca, Ill., where he is in charge of 10 engineers and technicians.

"A lot of people wonder how I can handle 10 people in my full-time job," he says, "and then in my part-time job, I handle 2,400."

He's treated a little differently in Iraq than he is back at the office.

For starters, he has a six-person security team that follows him everywhere.

"I want to do something special for them when we are done," he says. "Sometimes, when I think about everything, I'm in awe."

A FEW DAYS after Saddam Hussein's statue fell in

Baghdad, Machut is sitting behind his desk at the far end of a big green tent. The war is winding down — quicker than the Marines expected — and he's planning for what comes next.

His battalion will continue to supply the Marines with fuel and water.

At the same time, some of Machut's battalion put down the hose reel system; others built a water filtration center, turning canal water into drinking water. Machut also was in charge of that project, but it wasn't nearly as complicated.

His battalion could be used to help the Iraqis rebuild their country.

"We'll probably get involved in some humanitarian assistance projects," Machut says. "At the same time, we'll try to wrap things up in getting out of here."

He hopes to be home by October.

"There is a lot of work yet to do, and it's gonna be hard to keep people motivated because their thoughts are somewhere else," he says. "Everyone is starting to think about the parades back home and seeing the wives and kids and the vacations. Everyone is thinking about going home. But everyone knows we have a lot of work."

The Army has built a fixed hose to replace the Marines' soft hose, so it won't be so susceptible to attack.

"We have to pick up all these fuel bags," Machut says. "We have to clean them. We have to clean all our gear. We have to do all the maintenance on them and put them on ships that started coming here as early as last October."

He expects a difficult summer. The heat. The bugs. And the misery of being away from home.

But he's excited about the chance to help rebuild Iraq.

"We offer such a vast capability with our engineering assets," Machut says. "So much of the infrastructure has to be rebuilt. We'll probably start on some of the immediate needs before the Army can come in here with more deliberate actions."

His battalion may do road repair and some minor building repairs in Iraq.

"We can provide mobile electric power," Machut says. "These things will be real important to the surrounding communities.

"What's unique about the 6th ESB, of course, is we have all the civilian trades. We have guys who work as plumbers or electricians or steelworkers. There is a lot we offer that we can provide. Hopefully, they'll tap into us, and we'll be able to give that little extra."

HE LEANS BACK, CONTENT. A bunch of reservists pulled it off.

They made a little dot in a line that stretched from the White House to Baghdad.

"It's hard to describe how satisfied I am," he says. "I knew we would be a success. I came here with that attitude. So many other people didn't know if we would. They wondered about the reserves. Would we be ready? Would we have the skills? We have proven that in spades. We have gone far and above what everybody thought we would do. I'm terribly proud of my Marines. This is the chance of a lifetime, to lead a battalion into combat.

"I'm the luckiest man in the Marine Corps."

THE SERIES AND THE BOOK

For three months, Free Press writer Jeff Seidel and artist Richard Johnson covered the war in Iraq for the Detroit Free Press and Knight Ridder newspapers by telling the stories of individuals — military personnel and civilians. They filed reports from four countries — Qatar, Bahrain, Kuwait and Iraq — and from aboard the USS Abraham Lincoln. They embedded with the 1st Marine Expeditionary Force, 6th Engineer Support Battalion.

ABOUT THE WRITER

Jeff Seidel

Jeff Seidel, 36, is a staff writer at the Detroit Free Press. He is a three-time finalist for the Livingston Award and won a Sigma Delta Chi award in feature writing in 2003. Before joining the Free Press, Seidel was a sportswriter for 10 years. He covered the Minnesota Vikings for the St. Paul Pioneer Press from 1997-99. He lives in West Bloomfield, Mich., with his wife, Teresa, and three children, Jacob, Emma and Nick.

ABOUT THE ARTIST

Richard Johnson

Richard Johnson, 37, was born in Falkirk, Scotland, and had formal artist training in Dundee, Scotland. He joined the Free Press in 2000. Johnson was introduced to the crafts of drawing, fly fishing, bird watching and slapstick comedy by his grandfather, Herbert William Bingham, who died in 2001. Johnson maintains that drawing is infinitely easier than actually working for a living. He has two children, Sarah, 16, and Joe, 8, and is engaged to Karen Joseph, one of the copy editors of this book. They will be married in Scotland in 2004.